TARGET Bodybuilding

PER A. TESCH, PhD

Human Kinetics

Library of Congress Cataloging-in-Publication Data

Tesch, Per
Target bodybuilding / Per A. Tesch.
p. cm.
ISBN 0-88011-938-1
1. Bodybuilding. 2. Weight training. 3. Muscle strength.
I. Title.
GV546.5.T47 1999
646.7'5--dc21 98-40334
CIP

ISBN: 0-88011-938-1

Developmental Editor: Kent Reel; **Assistant Editors:** Rebecca Crist, Coree Schutter, and Leigh Lahood; **Copyeditor:** Marc Jennings; **Proofreader:** Ann Bruehler; **Graphic Designer:** Robert Reuther; **Graphic Artist:** Tara Welsch; **Cover Designer:** Jack Davis; **Photographer (cover):** Per Bernal; **Photographer (interior):** Per Bernal; **Models:** Lisbeth Wikström, Swedish Champion and Stephan Haertl, M.Sc, European and German Heavyweight Champion; **Printer:** United Graphics

Human Kinetics books are available at special discounts for bulk purchase. Special editions or book excerpts can also be created to specification. For details, contact the Special Sales Manager at Human Kinetics.

Printed in the United States of America 10 9 8 7 6 5 4 3 2 1

Human Kinetics
Web site: http://www.humankinetics.com/

United States: Human Kinetics, P.O. Box 5076, Champaign, IL 61825-5076
1-800-747-4457
e-mail: humank@hkusa.com

Canada: Human Kinetics, 475 Devonshire Road Unit 100, Windsor, ON N8Y 2L5
1-800-465-7301 (in Canada only)
e-mail: humank@hkcanada.com

Europe: Human Kinetics, P.O. Box IW14, Leeds LS16 6TR, United Kingdom
(44) 1132 781708
e-mail: humank@hkeurope.com

Australia: Human Kinetics, 57A Price Avenue, Lower Mitcham, South Australia 5062
(088) 277 1555
e-mail: humank@hkaustralia.com

New Zealand: Human Kinetics, P.O. Box 105-231, Auckland 1
(09) 523 3462
e-mail: humank@hknewz.com

CONTENTS

CHAPTER 1

MUSCLES AND MRI

WOULDN'T IT BE GREAT TO BE ABLE TO LOOK INSIDE YOUR ARM and see which of the three heads of the triceps brachii (the elbow extensor muscle group) is used in the military press? This book shows you that the long head is not used to do the military press! You know the best way to stress the soleus muscle in the back of the calf is to do seated calf raises. Now you can see why. Would you believe that the hamstring muscles in the back of the thigh are not really the ones stretched as you lower into that deep squat? It is really the powerful adductor muscles of the thigh that are pulled, and you will see this. In this book, you will see which specific exercises for the arms and legs can be used to develop individual muscles—and even *parts* of them—like never before. If you want to train smartly do the right exercises for specific muscles, and see which different exercises can and cannot be used to train those specific muscles, then this is the book for you.

What does this book provide that is so new? Why is it different from the 50 or so other bodybuilding books on the market? A powerful technology, magnetic resonance imaging (MRI), was used to definitively show you which individual muscles are worked in different bodybuilding exercises. No more guesswork based on where a muscle starts and stops: "Oh, it goes across this joint, so it must do this." No, this book is much different.

MRI is the most advanced technology available today for visualization of soft tissue inside the human body. An MRI image of the left upper arm shows individual muscles with remarkable clarity (figure 1).

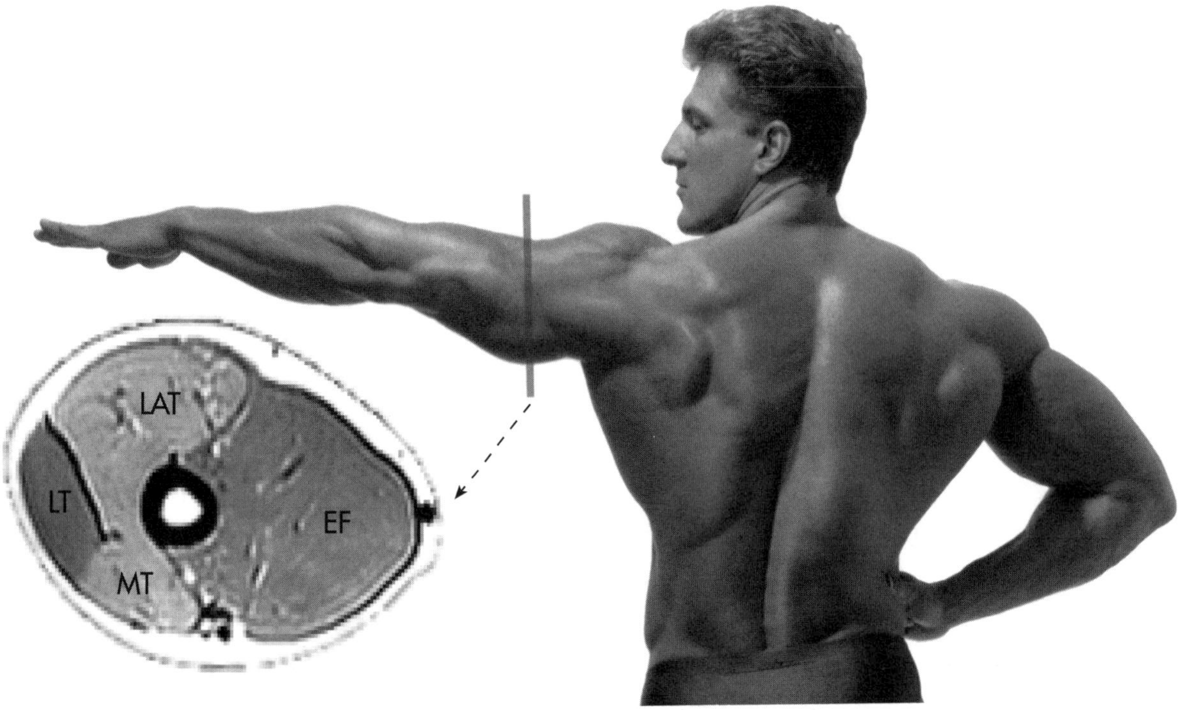

Figure 1 Native MRI of the upper arm.

This MRI is a slice taken where the line is drawn across the bodybuilder's left upper arm. To get oriented to the image, hold your left arm out like he does, and imagine looking into a slice of it. The large vein that runs down the middle of your biceps is evident on the right side of the image as a black dot. In the middle of the image, there is a black doughnut-shaped object. This is the bone of your upper arm, the humerus. Now look at the muscle tissue! The elbow flexors (EF) are on the right side of the humerus and appear dark gray. The long head (LT) of the triceps brachii appears on the far right of the image and is also dark gray. The lateral (LAT) and medial (MT) heads of the triceps brachii, however, are much lighter. They are "lit up" because this MRI of the left upper arm was taken after the bodybuilder had performed five sets of ten repetitions of the military press with a load that gave a pretty good pump. While the physiological reason for this difference in contrast, this change in color, is not known, it's accepted that this occurred because these two heads of the triceps brachii were used to do the exercise. The long head (LT) was not used and remained dark gray, even though this exercise requires considerable elbow extension. The elbow flexors (EF) were also not used—and remained dark gray—because they do not help with elbow extension. The take-home message is that you cannot use the military press to train the long head of the triceps brachii.

I've divided the pattern and extent of muscle use into three levels of gray for the remainder of the book, so you can easily see the most important thing: which individual muscles are used to do a given exercise. Light gray means the muscle worked hard during the exercise, medium gray indicates moderate involvement, and dark gray means the muscle was not used. When shades of gray are applied to the muscles in Figure 1, the *lateral* and *medial* heads of the triceps brachii appear light gray because they are really taxed by the military press (figure 2). The *long* head and the forearm flexors are shaded dark because they contribute little to this exercise. No muscles appear medium gray in this image because none were moderately involved in this exercise.

This is the first report, using the state-of-the-art technology of MRI, to show in detail which muscles do the work in the most important arm and leg exercises bodybuilders perform. Experienced bodybuilders performed a variety of common exercises to the level of getting a good pump—five sets of ten to twelve repetitions. Then, using magnetic resonance imaging, it was possible to "look inside" their bodies to see which muscles were used to do the exercise. You'll see a concentration on exercises for the back and front of the upper arm, thigh, and calf. You won't find coverage of every arm and leg exercise ever used in bodybuilding, but you will see many of the more common ones.

HOW THE TECHNIQUE WORKS

Regardless of whether you use weight training for muscle toning, rehabilitation, or hardcore bodybuilding, you need to know which muscles are used in a particular movement or exercise. The action and functional use of different skeletal muscles is described in detail in almost any standard textbook of anatomy. Such information, published and available early in the twentieth century, is invaluable and has been the foundation for developing exercise routines used in the weight room over the years. Today, monthly muscle and fitness magazines describe muscle involvement in established or more novel and complex exercises. Such information shall not be ignored, but is often based on personal experience rather than scientific evaluation. More objective information on muscle use is

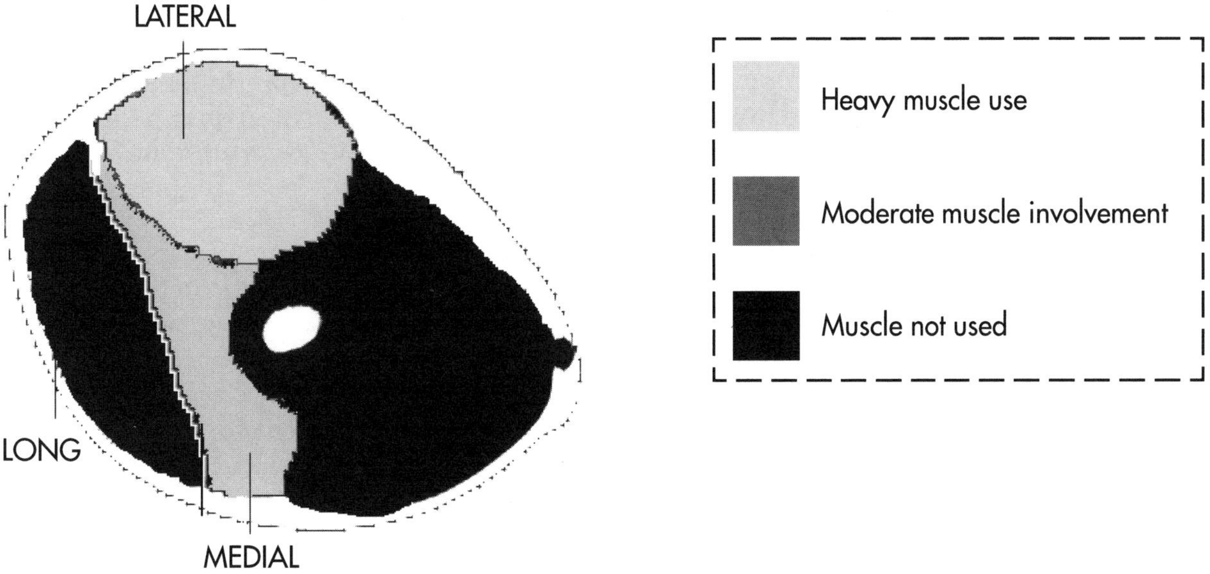

Figure 2

available through electromyography (EMG), which measures the electrical activity of a muscle. It's well established that EMG activity increases in a linear fashion with increased load or muscle force. Unfortunately, though, this technique has limitations. EMG recordings using surface electrodes are limited to superficial muscles, and insertion of needle or wire electrodes into muscles complicates measurements during dynamic exercise—not to mention being uncomfortable for the subject. Other serious problems with this technique include quantification of muscle use and so-called crosstalk between adjacent muscles. Magnetic resonance imaging is the most advanced technology available today for visualization of soft tissue inside the human body. Hence, MRI is an important clinical tool in diagnosing disease. But it's also been proven useful in evaluating muscle use during exercise. In the late '80s, researchers using MRI found that muscles that had performed contractile activity showed a contrast shift; those involved became lighter in images obtained immediately after exercise, and muscles not used remained dark gray, as before exercise. An example of this response is shown in Figure 1. In the native image, a slice taken of the upper left arm where the vertical line is drawn, the lateral (LAT) and medial (MT) heads of the triceps brachii are markedly lighter than the long head (LT) of the triceps muscle or the elbow flexors (EF) to the right of the bone. This is because a previous exercise routine involved the medial and lateral heads. This exercise-induced change remains for some time after exercise and then fades away. Within an hour after the exercise, muscles will again show normal contrast in an image; they'll all appear dark gray. The subcutaneous fat that surrounds the muscles is white and the bone appears black. It was also possible to quantitate the extent of use by measuring the exercise-induced contrast shift expressed as spin-spin relaxation time (T_2). Experiments clearly showed that the change was dependent on the intensity of exercise, because the heavier the load lifted, the greater the increase in T_2. Moreover, in studies where the exercise-induced contrast shift was measured and muscular activity recorded by surface electrode EMG from the superficial biceps brachii muscles, it was shown that increases in EMG activity and T_2 changes in individual muscles correlated strongly. Another study described in detail the use of individual muscles in the parallel barbell squat. The technique has also been employed in research studies aimed at mapping individual muscle use in exercises typical of shoulder and neck rehabilitation programs. Although we don't know what causes this exercise-induced contrast shift phenomenon, it's obvious that MRI is an exceptional tool for studying muscle use during exercise.

APPLYING THE TECHNIQUE

The information in this book describing muscle use during weight training is based on hundreds of experiments. The exercises examined involve muscles of the front and back of the upper arm, the thigh, and the calf. Although all subjects were accustomed to these exercises, they were thoroughly instructed on how to execute each using correct movement technique. For each exercise routine, three or four experienced male and female weight trainees performed five sets of 10-12 repetitions to failure. If they failed to maintain proper form, exercise was stopped and weights were reduced. The subjects rested for 90 seconds between sets. After each exercise, they rested one hour to ensure that the contrast shift returned to normal before the next exercise. Subjects were examined with a General Electric 1.5-T superconducting magnet four to five minutes after completing the last set of each exercise. Multiple transaxial images one centimeter thick with a one-half cm gap between slices were obtained along the axis of the lower leg, the thigh, or the upper arm. Ink marks were made at the level of interest and aligned with cross hairs of the imager. Braces were applied to standardize positioning in the magnet bore over repeated scans. Two T_2-weighted images (2,000 milliseconds repetition time; 30 and 60 ms echo time) were collected within a 40- or 20-cm field of view body or 25-cm diameter extremity coil. A 256 x 256 or 256 x 128 matrix was acquired with one excitation. Total collection time was 4-5 minutes. Magnetic resonance images were transferred to a Macintosh computer for subsequent analyses. Because the exercise-induced contrast shift is similar along the length of the muscle, only one image, at the level indicated by the line drawn in the pictures, was examined from each experiment.

The exercise-induced contrast shift was then subjectively rated using a semiquantitative approach. The pattern and extent of use was subsequently partitioned into three shades of gray. Light gray signifies that heavy use was required during the exercise, medium gray indicates moderate muscle involvement, and dark denotes no muscle use. The results presented here are uniform among subjects. The results from analyses of the native images have been displayed in computer-created muscle cross sections of the upper arm, the thigh, and the calf. For each chapter, the results are presented using this standard cross section.

Sit back, relax and enjoy this remarkable visual journey inside the human body to see what your muscles do. Good training.

MAKING SENSE OF THE MRIS

To use this book effectively to target muscles, it's essential to understand how the MRI images are oriented to the body. The following section shows how to read the MRIs of each body region covered in the book. The shaded line through the model's arm or leg indicates the cross section where the MRI image was taken.

BACK AND FRONT OF UPPER ARM

Raise your left arm beside your body, palm down, and imagine looking into a cross-sectional slice of it. Always view the images from this perspective. If the bodybuilder is facing you while doing the exercise, just put yourself in his/her place and visualize the image being taken of your left upper arm.

UPPER ARM GUIDE

Lateral, long, and *medial* heads of the triceps brachii and the *elbow flexors* of the biceps brachii and brachialis muscles.

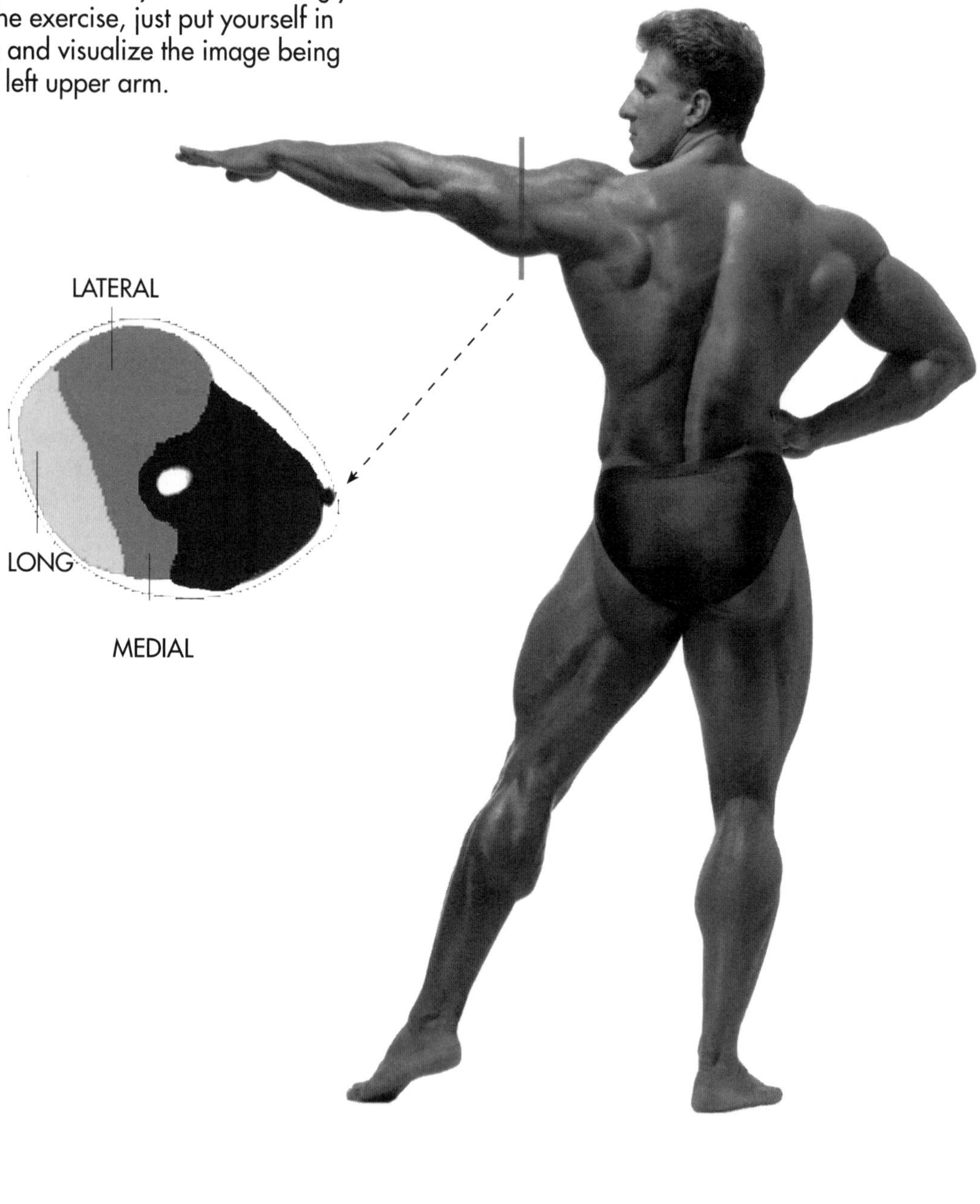

THIGH

Stand, look down at your right leg, and imagine looking into a cross-sectional slice of your right thigh. If the bodybuilder is facing you while doing the exercise, just put yourself in his/her place and visualize the image being taken of your right thigh.

THIGH GUIDE

AD B = Adductor brevis
AD L = Adductor longus
AD M = Adductor magnus
BF = Biceps femoris
GR = Gracilis
RF = Rectus femoris
SR = Sartorius
ST = Semitendinosus
VM = Vastus medialis
VL = Vastus lateralis
VI = Vastus intermedius

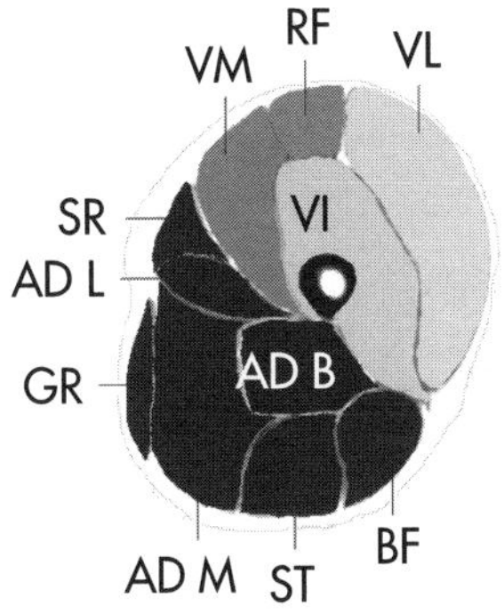

continued

MAKING SENSE OF THE MRIS *(continued)*

CALF

Stand, look down at your left leg, and imagine looking into a cross-sectional slice of your left calf. If the bodybuilder is facing you while doing the exercise, just put yourself in his/her place and visualize the image being taken of your left calf.

CALF GUIDE

SO = Soleus
MG = Medial gastrocnemius
LG = Lateral gastrocnemius
TA = Tibialis anterior
TP = Tibialis posterior
PO = Popliteus
EDL = Extensor digitorum longus
PL = Peroneus longus

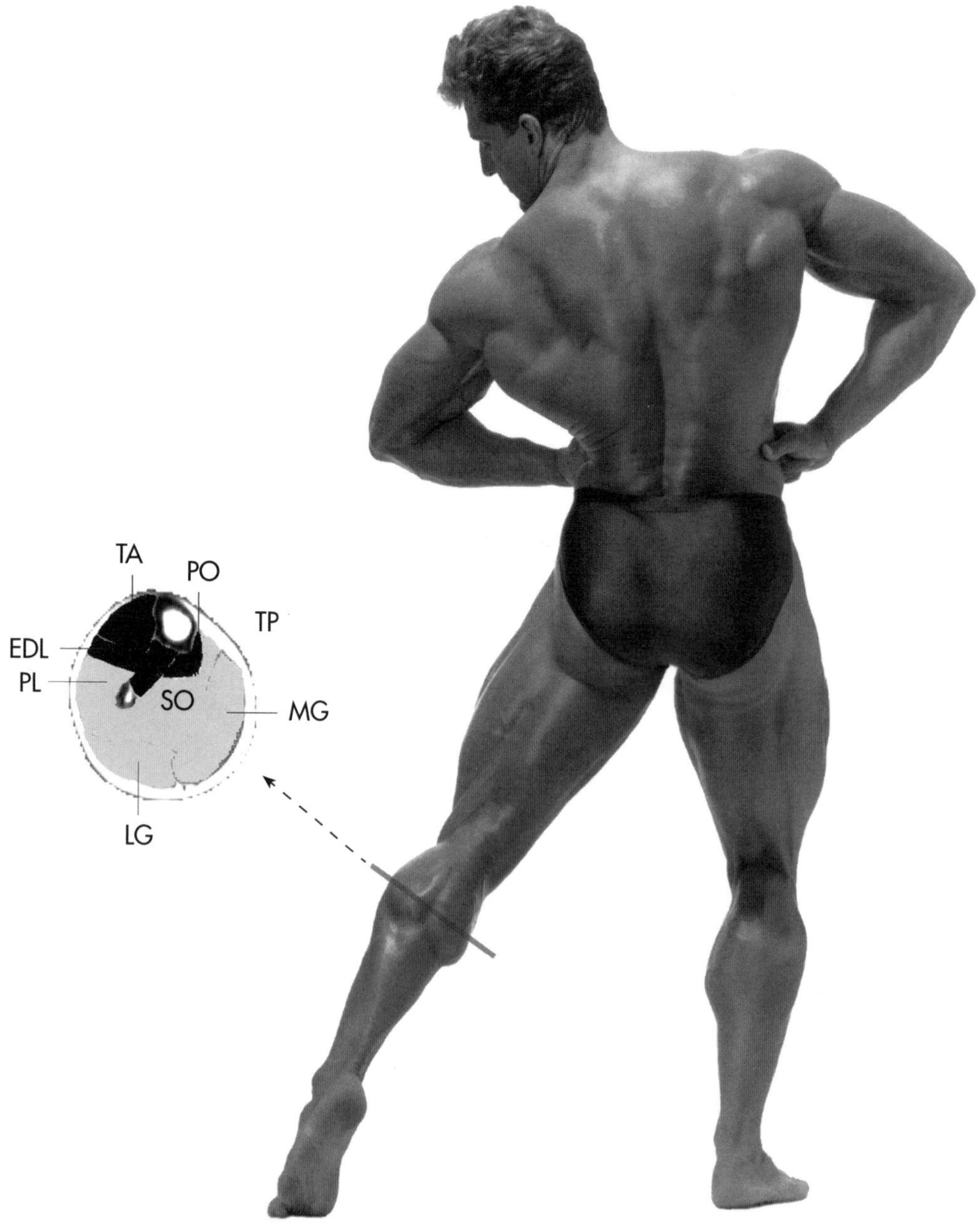

CHAPTER 2

FRONT OF UPPER ARM

THE MRI SCANS SHOW THAT SEVERAL STANDING OR SEATED dumbbell or barbell curls involve simultaneous heavy use of the medial and lateral aspects of the biceps brachii with some support from the brachialis (see, for example, exercises 5, 6, 8, and 9). The standing biceps curl with straight bar and arm blaster (exercise 10) or with narrow grip (exercise 11) use all three heads heavily and should be used in every biceps program. Performing dumbbell curls with neutral grip will limit involvement of the medial head (as in exercises 4 and 7). Optimal stress of the medial head, to build the "top" of the biceps, is achieved by using exercises with grip and/or lateral rotation (for example, exercises 1-3). To help you target the biceps, the chart at the end of the chapter shows which heads are stressed in each exercise.

1

STANDING BICEPS CURL

With Straight Bar and Wide Grip

A

TECHNIQUE

This is one of the classics, so the execution of this exercise should be familiar to you. Start the exercise with the bar resting on your thighs and your torso erect. Smoothly curl the bar, raising it as far as possible, and after a slight pause, lower it to the starting position. It is crucial to keep your torso stationary. Also, keep your elbows in one place as the bar ascends and then descends.

B

STANDING BICEPS CURL

With Straight Bar and Wide Grip

MUSCLE FUNCTION

Not surprising. All three of the major arm flexors are involved in this exercise. The brunt of the load is taken by the medial head of the biceps brachii. The lateral or long head of the biceps and the brachialis make a moderate contribution to performing these curls.

The triceps brachii muscle of the back of the upper arm appears black because it does not contribute in this exercise.

- Heavy muscle use
- Moderate muscle involvement
- Muscle not used

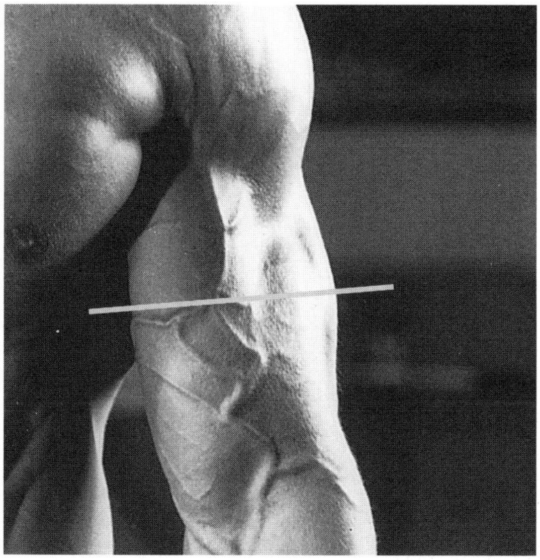

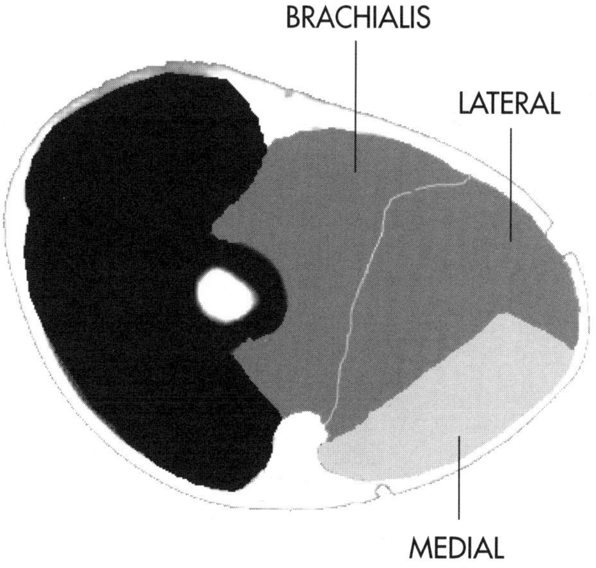

To understand the orientation of the MRI, raise your left arm beside your body, palm down, and imagine looking into a cross-sectional slice of it. The cross-section of the MRI is indicated by the bar in the photo.

2

STANDING BICEPS CURL

With EZ Bar and Wide Grip

A

TECHNIQUE

This exercise is comparable to exercise 1 except that an EZ curl bar is used. With a wide grip on the EZ curl bar, the hands are about shoulder width apart and the palms slightly rotated as compared to the grip used with the straight bar.

B

STANDING BICEPS CURL

With EZ Bar and Wide Grip

MUSCLE FUNCTION

The slight rotation of the hand inward to grasp the EZ bar as compared to the straight bar does not seem to alter muscle use in standing curls with a wide grip. The medial head of the biceps brachii is really taxed, while the lateral head and the brachialis pitch in to do some of the work.

The triceps brachii muscle of the back of the upper arm appears black because it does not contribute in this exercise.

(light)	Heavy muscle use
(gray)	Moderate muscle involvement
(black)	Muscle not used

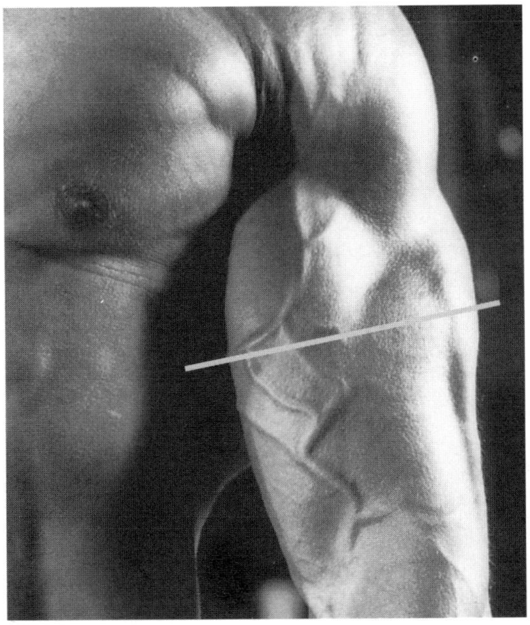

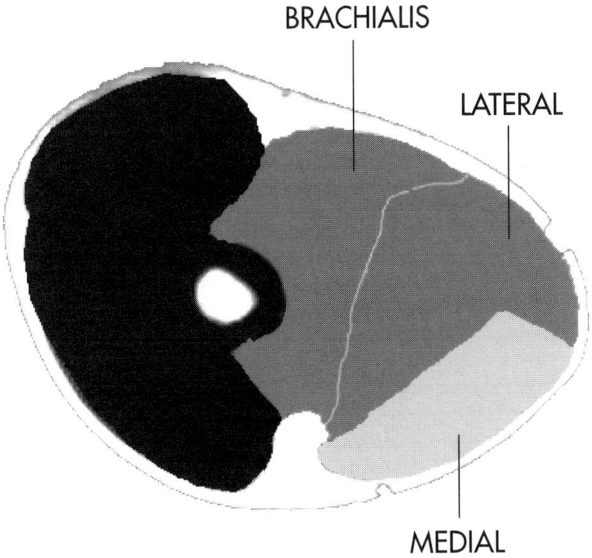

To understand the orientation of the MRI, raise your left arm beside your body, palm down, and imagine looking into a cross-sectional slice of it. The cross-section of the MRI is indicated by the bar in the photo.

3

STANDING DUMBBELL CURL

With Palm Up

A

TECHNIQUE

This is essentially the same as exercise 1 except that dumbbells are used instead of the straight bar. You can perform this exercise using one or two dumbbells at a time. Remember, keep your palm up, and your elbow and torso stationary.

B

STANDING DUMBBELL CURL

With Palm Up

MUSCLE FUNCTION

Standing dumbbell curls with the palm up really tax the medial head of the biceps brachii, with some involvement of the lateral head and the brachialis.

The triceps brachii muscle of the back of the upper arm appears black because it does not contribute in this exercise.

Heavy muscle use

Moderate muscle involvement

Muscle not used

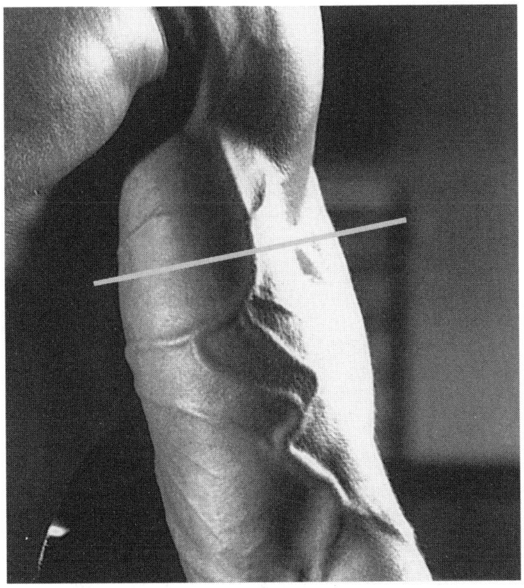

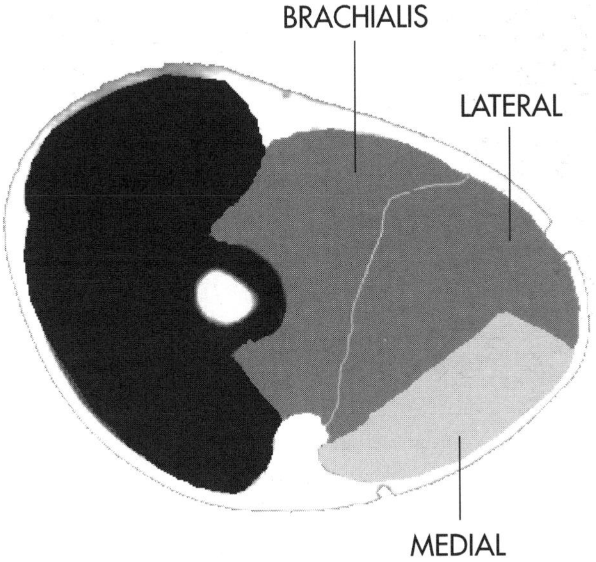

To understand the orientation of the MRI, raise your left arm beside your body, palm down, and imagine looking into a cross-sectional slice of it. The cross-section of the MRI is indicated by the bar in the photo.

4

STANDING DUMBBELL CURL

With Neutral Grip

A

TECHNIQUE

This is just like exercise 3 except for the grip. In the neutral position, the dumbbells are held so the palms are toward the body throughout the range of motion.

B

STANDING DUMBBELL CURL

With Neutral Grip

MUSCLE FUNCTION

Things are starting to be different now. The lateral head does the brunt of the work. The medial head and the brachialis are only moderately involved.

The triceps brachii muscle of the back of the upper arm appears black because it does not contribute in this exercise.

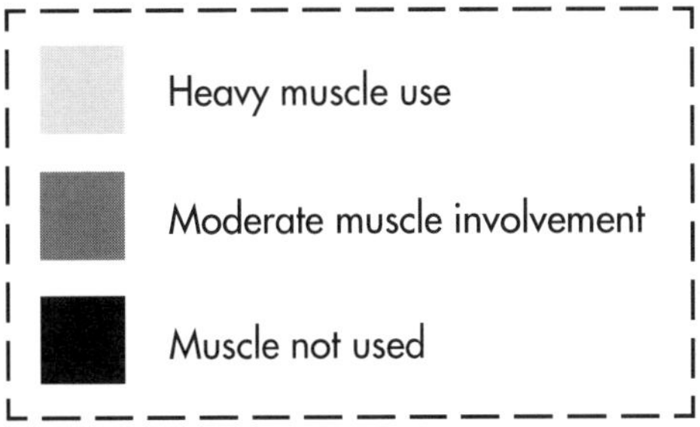

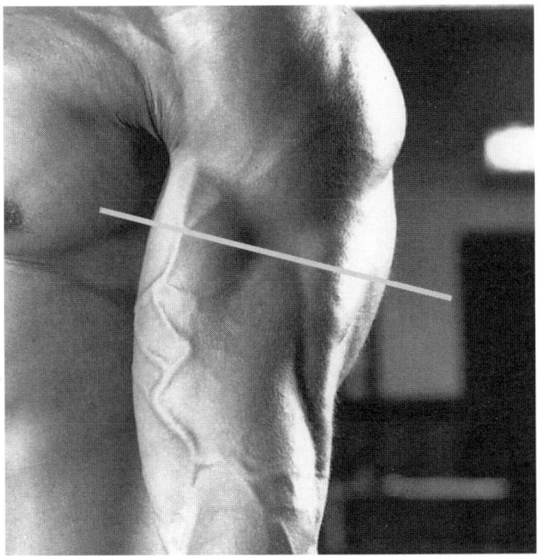

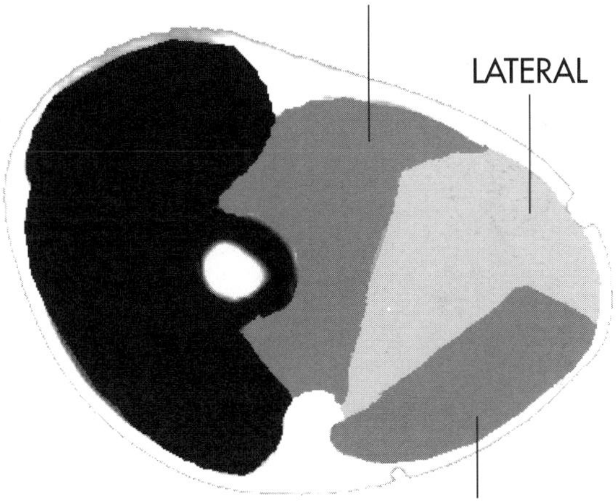

To understand the orientation of the MRI, raise your left arm beside your body, palm down, and imagine looking into a cross-sectional slice of it. The cross-section of the MRI is indicated by the bar in the photo.

5

STANDING DUMBBELL CURL

With Lateral Rotation

A

TECHNIQUE

This is a combination of exercises 3 and 4. Start with the dumbbells held in the neutral position. As you raise the weight, however, rotate your palms out so that at the end of the range of motion, your thumbs point away from your body.

B

STANDING DUMBBELL CURL

With Lateral Rotation

MUSCLE FUNCTION

What would you expect if you did curls by starting in the neutral position and rotating the palms up as you raised the load? Both heads of the biceps brachii enjoy severe stress. This is not the case for the brachialis, which again shows moderate use.

The triceps brachii muscle of the back of the upper arm appears black because it does not contribute in this exercise.

- Heavy muscle use
- Moderate muscle involvement
- Muscle not used

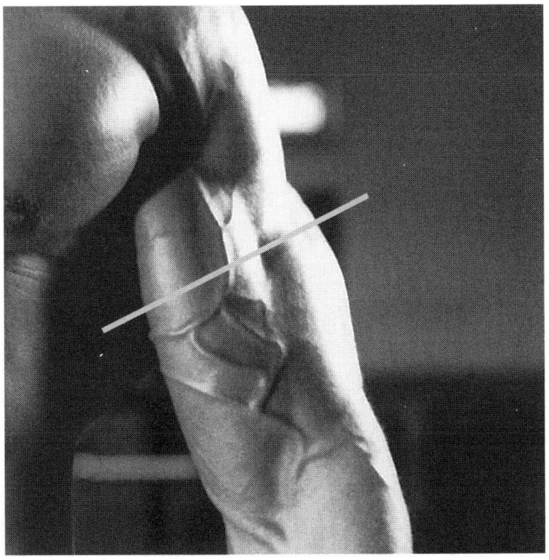

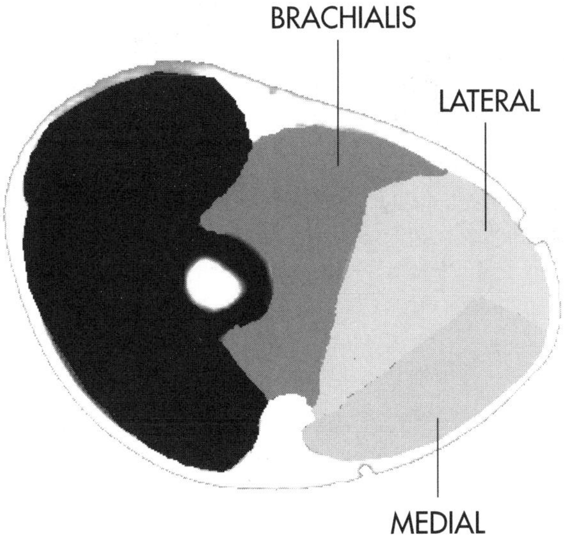

To understand the orientation of the MRI, raise your left arm beside your body, palm down, and imagine looking into a cross-sectional slice of it. The cross-section of the MRI is indicated by the bar in the photo.

6 INCLINE SEATED DUMBBELL CURL

With Lateral Rotation

A

TECHNIQUE

This is executed just like exercise 5, the standing dumbbell curl with lateral rotation, except you are sitting on a bench. Remember, keep your upper body stationary and feel that stretch.

B

INCLINE SEATED DUMBBELL CURL

With Lateral Rotation

MUSCLE FUNCTION

This exercise stresses both heads of the biceps brachii with less support from the brachialis.

The triceps brachii muscle of the back of the upper arm appears black because it does not contribute in this exercise.

(light)	Heavy muscle use
(gray)	Moderate muscle involvement
(black)	Muscle not used

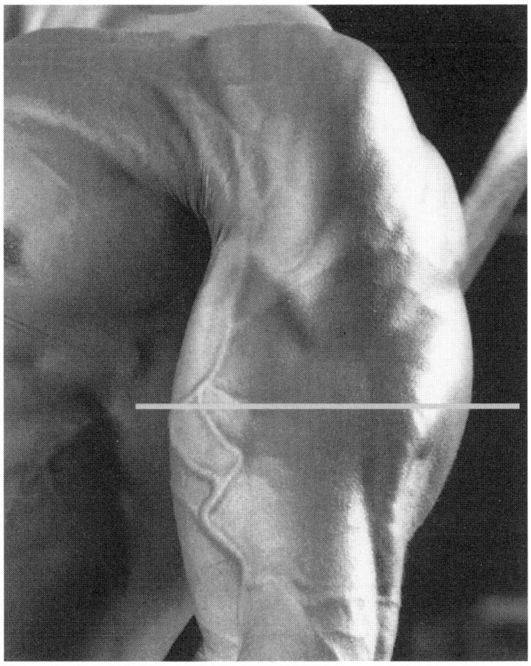

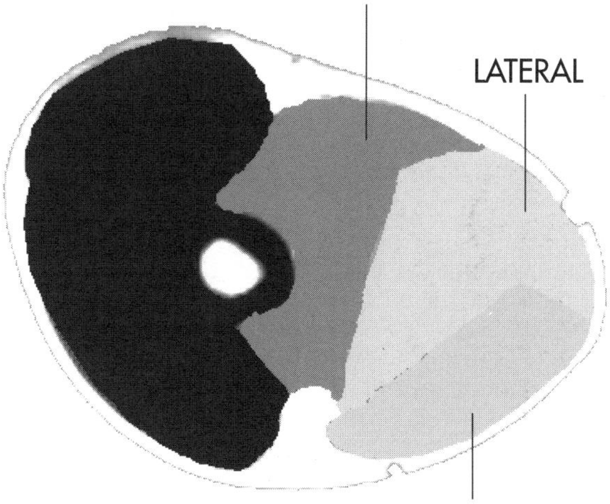

To understand the orientation of the MRI, raise your left arm beside your body, palm down, and imagine looking into a cross-sectional slice of it. The cross-section of the MRI is indicated by the bar in the photo.

7

INCLINE SEATED DUMBBELL CURL

With Neutral Grip

A

TECHNIQUE

This is just like exercise 6, except that the hands remain in the neutral position (palms toward the body) throughout the range of motion.

B

INCLINE SEATED DUMBBELL CURL

With Neutral Grip

MUSCLE FUNCTION

By keeping a neutral grip throughout the range of motion, you really stress the lateral head of the biceps brachii and the brachialis. The medial head is only moderately involved.

The triceps brachii muscle of the back of the upper arm appears black because it does not contribute in this exercise.

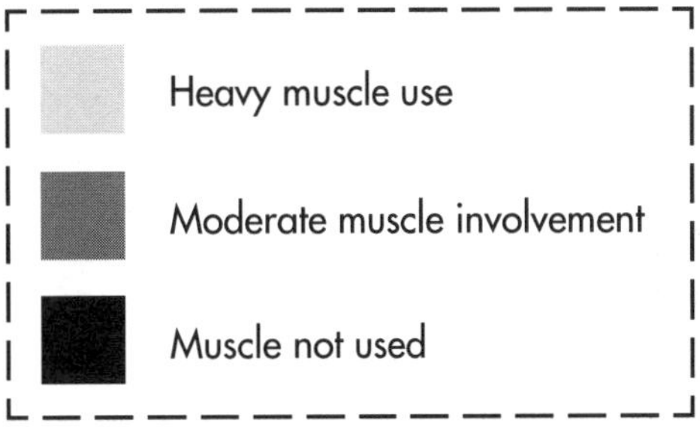

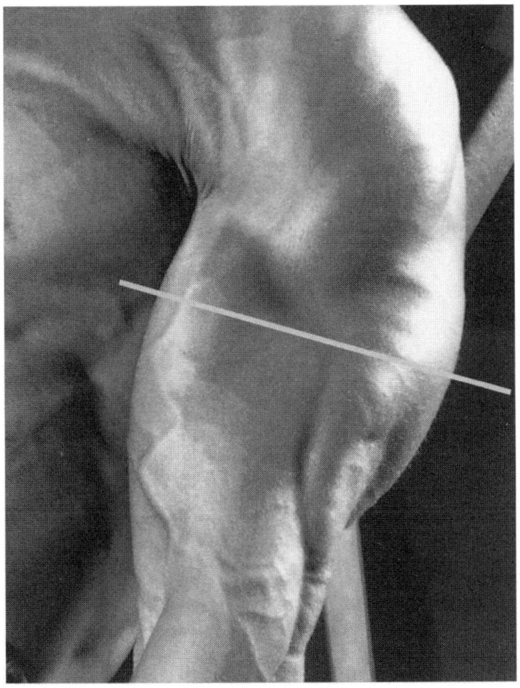

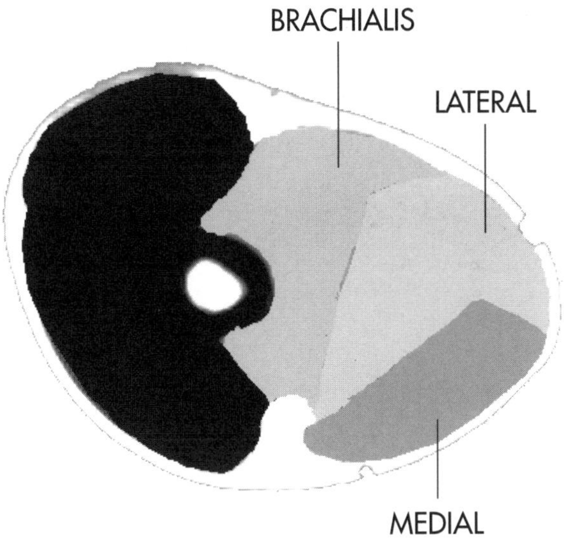

To understand the orientation of the MRI, raise your left arm beside your body, palm down, and imagine looking into a cross-sectional slice of it. The cross-section of the MRI is indicated by the bar in the photo.

8

INCLINE SEATED DUMBBELL CURL

With Palm Up

A

TECHNIQUE

This is just like exercise 7, except that the hands are held palm up throughout the range of motion.

B

INCLINE SEATED DUMBBELL CURL

With Palm Up

MUSCLE FUNCTION

With the palm up throughout the range of motion, both heads of the biceps brachii are maximally stressed. The brachialis shows less involvement.

The triceps brachii muscle of the back of the upper arm appears black because it does not contribute in this exercise.

- Heavy muscle use
- Moderate muscle involvement
- Muscle not used

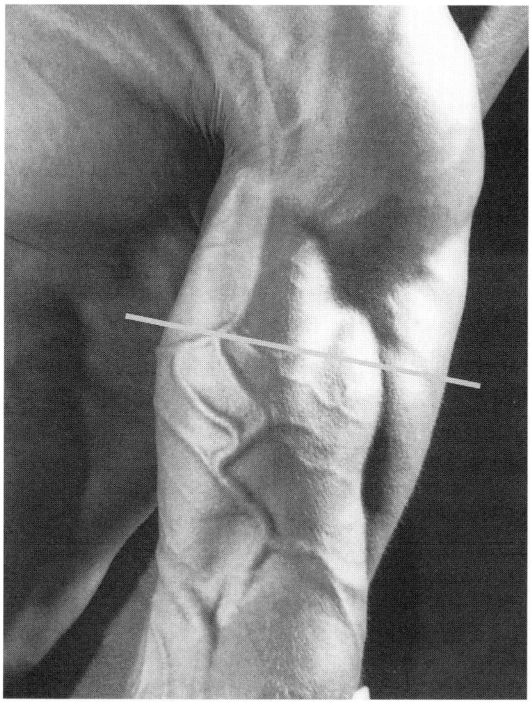

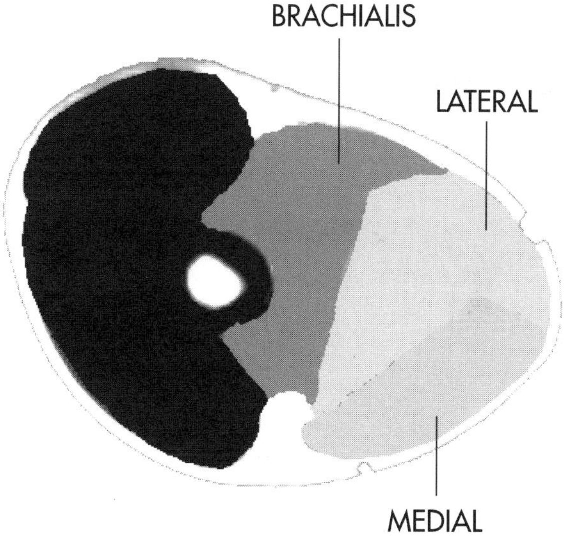

To understand the orientation of the MRI, raise your left arm beside your body, palm down, and imagine looking into a cross-sectional slice of it. The cross-section of the MRI is indicated by the bar in the photo.

9

STANDING BICEPS CURL

With EZ Bar and Arm Blaster

A

TECHNIQUE

This is just like exercise 2 except it is done using an arm blaster. This really isolates the biceps. You can get similar isolation by bracing your arm(s) against an incline bench (preacher curl). Be careful when lowering the weight; the excellent isolation could lead you to hyperextend your elbows at the bottom of the bar's descent.

B

STANDING BICEPS CURL

With EZ Bar and Arm Blaster

MUSCLE FUNCTION

The medial and lateral heads of the biceps brachii are really put into action. The brachialis is involved somewhat less.

The triceps brachii muscle of the back of the upper arm appears black because it does not contribute in this exercise.

- Heavy muscle use
- Moderate muscle involvement
- Muscle not used

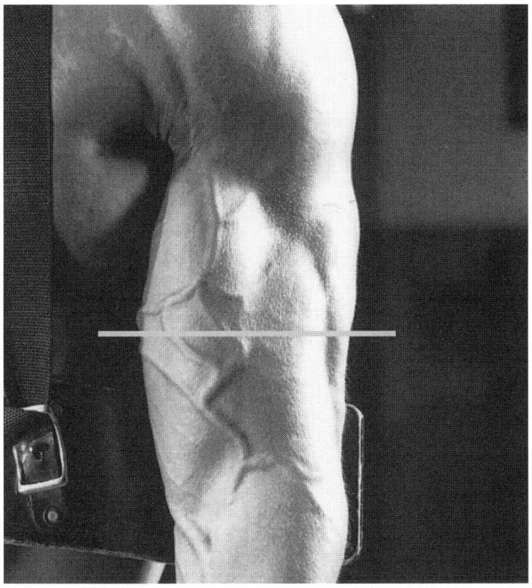

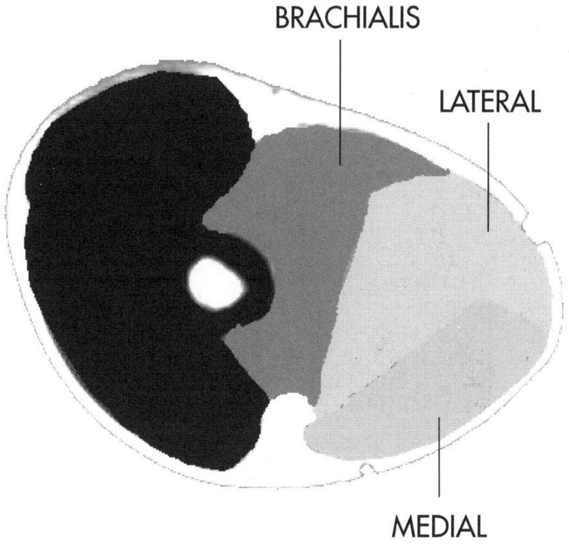

To understand the orientation of the MRI, raise your left arm beside your body, palm down, and imagine looking into a cross-sectional slice of it. The cross-section of the MRI is indicated by the bar in the photo.

10

STANDING BICEPS CURL

With Straight Bar and Arm Blaster

A

TECHNIQUE

This is just like exercise 9, except a straight bar is used. Again, you can use an incline bench instead of an arm blaster to isolate the biceps.

B

STANDING BICEPS CURL

With Straight Bar and Arm Blaster

MUSCLE FUNCTION

All three muscles in the front of those big guns get a chance to enjoy the utmost training stimulus—if you will just do it.

The triceps brachii muscle of the back of the upper arm appears black because it does not contribute in this exercise.

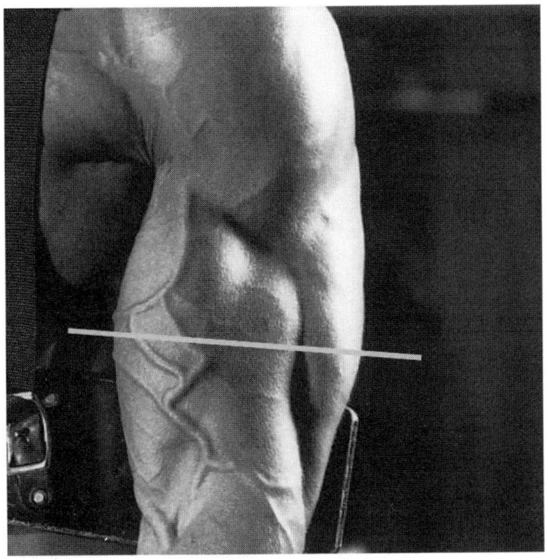

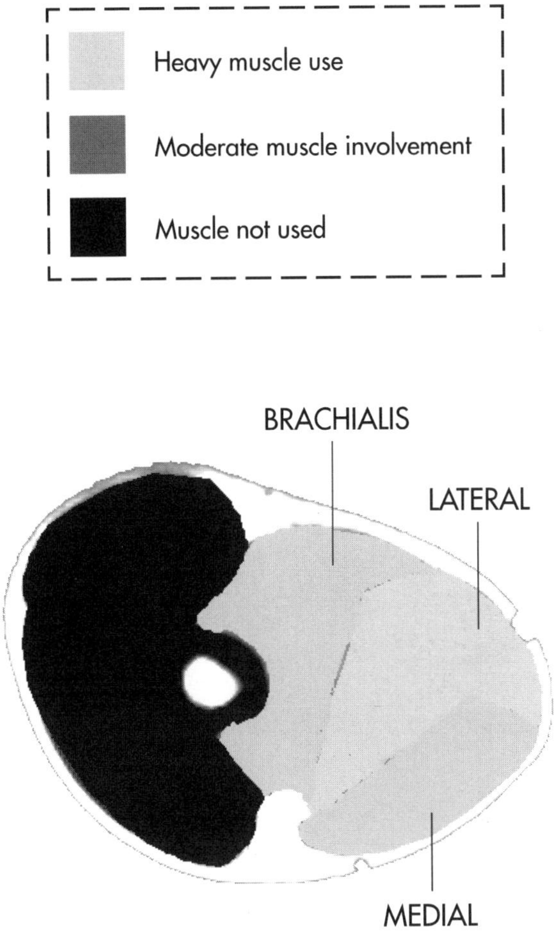

To understand the orientation of the MRI, raise your left arm beside your body, palm down, and imagine looking into a cross-sectional slice of it. The cross-section of the MRI is indicated by the bar in the photo.

11

STANDING BICEPS CURL

With Straight Bar and Narrow Grip

A

TECHNIQUE

This is like exercise 1 for the front of the upper arm, except a narrow grip is used.

B

STANDING BICEPS CURL

With Straight Bar and Narrow Grip

MUSCLE FUNCTION

Here, all three major elbow flexors get to enjoy a marked training stimulus. Compared to the wide-grip version of this exercise, the narrow grip seems a more natural movement that allows you to isolate the elbow flexors and eliminate extraneous movement more completely. As with exercise 10, this seems to really blast the fronts of the upper arms.

The triceps brachii muscle of the back of the upper arm appears black because it does not contribute in this exercise.

Heavy muscle use

Moderate muscle involvement

Muscle not used

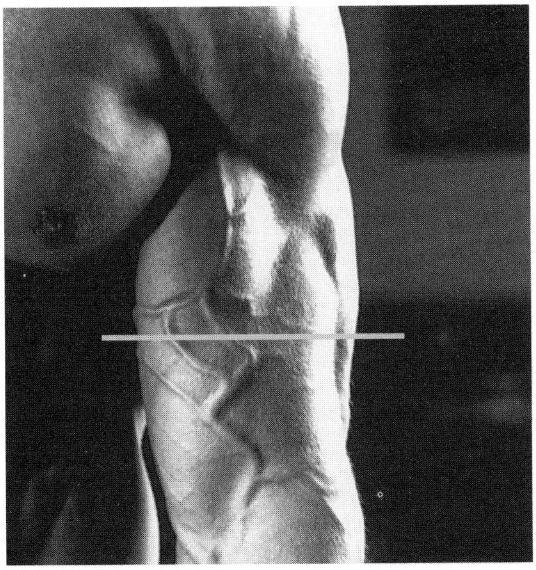

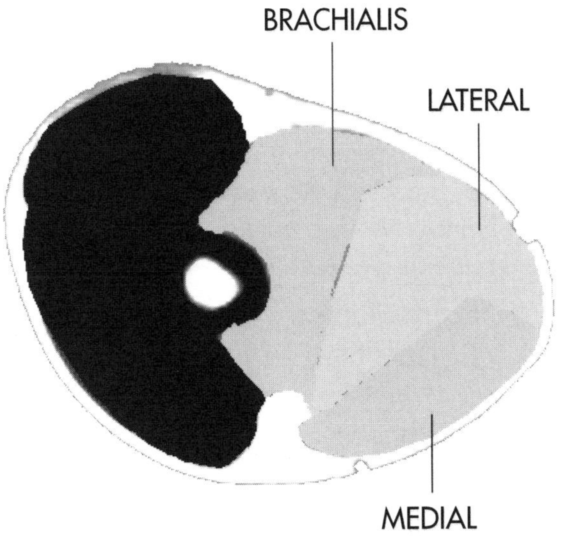

To understand the orientation of the MRI, raise your left arm beside your body, palm down, and imagine looking into a cross-sectional slice of it. The cross-section of the MRI is indicated by the bar in the photo.

MUSCLE USE GUIDE

Two Xs denote heavy muscle use; one X denotes moderate muscle involvement. No X is indicated for muscles that show no use during exercise.

FRONT OF THE UPPER ARM

	EXERCISE NAME	LAT	MED	BRA
#1	**Standing Biceps Curl** with straight bar and wide grip	X	XX	X
#2	**Standing Biceps Curl** with EZ bar and wide grip	X	XX	X
#3	**Standing Dumbbell Curl** with palm up	X	XX	X
#4	**Standing Dumbbell Curl** with neutral grip	XX	X	X
#5	**Standing Dumbbell Curl** with lateral rotation	XX	XX	X
#6	**Incline Seated Dumbbell Curl** with lateral rotation	XX	XX	X
#7	**Incline Seated Dumbbell Curl** with neutral grip	XX	X	XX
#8	**Incline Seated Dumbbell Curl** with palm up	XX	XX	X
#9	**Standing Biceps Curl** with EZ bar and arm blaster	XX	XX	X
#10	**Standing Biceps Curl** with straight bar and arm blaster	XX	XX	XX
#11	**Standing Biceps Curl** with straight bar and narrow grip	XX	XX	XX

CHAPTER 3

BACK OF UPPER ARM

AS THE MRI SCANS SHOW, SEVERAL EXERCISES OFFER HEAVY USE of all three heads of the triceps, particularly exercises 2, 4, 5, 9, 10, and 12. To target the long head of the triceps, try exercises 1, 6, and 17; the medial and lateral heads also help out in these exercises. The lateral head is highly stressed in exercises 3 and 13. The medial head appears to be hard to activate selectively. Once it is heavily involved, the lateral head is also heavily used, with all three heads brought into serious action. The chart on pages 74-75 will help you pinpoint the parts of the triceps muscle you want to develop.

FRENCH PRESS
With EZ Bar

A

TECHNIQUE

In the starting position, hold the EZ bar on the inside with arms extended directly over chest; the grip is midway between neutral and palm up. The bar is lowered to the forehead by flexing at the elbows, and after a short pause, raised to the starting position by extending at the elbows. This is not close grip benches or overhead flies, so keep the elbows stationary, held close together.

B

FRENCH PRESS

With EZ Bar

MUSCLE FUNCTION

The French press with an EZ bar places marked emphasis on the long of the triceps brachii. The medial and lateral heads of the triceps brachii are also important in this exercise, as indicated by their moderate use.

The muscles of the front of the upper arm appear black because they do not contribute in the exercise.

Heavy muscle use

Moderate muscle involvement

Muscle not used

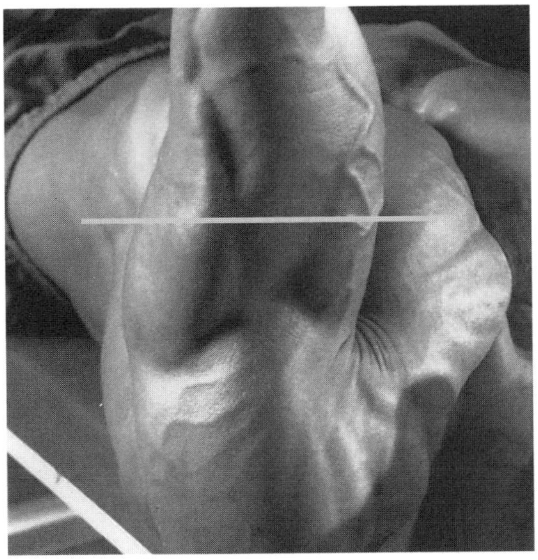

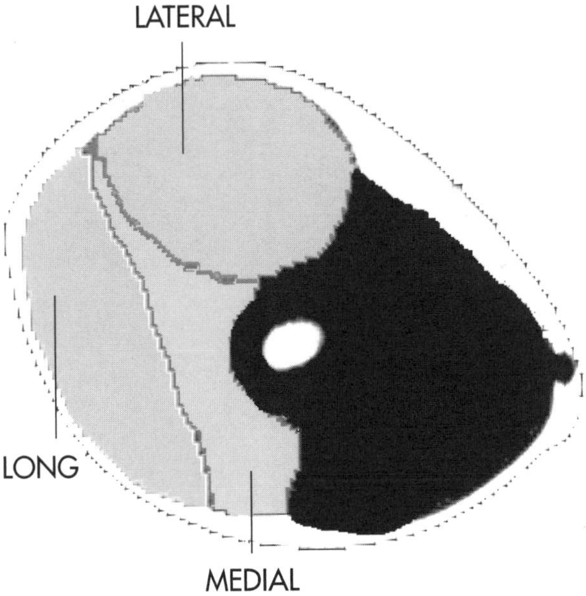

To understand the orientation of the MRI, raise your left arm beside your body, palm down, and imagine looking into a cross-sectional slice of it. The cross-section of the MRI is indicated by the bar in the photo.

2

FRENCH PRESS

With EZ Bar on Decline Bench

A

TECHNIQUE

This is similar to exercise 1, except that it is done on a decline bench. The feet are higher than the head, six inches in this example.

B

FRENCH PRESS

With EZ Bar on Decline Bench

MUSCLE FUNCTION

Doing the French press with an EZ bar in the decline position appears to allow for a greater range of motion about the elbow joint, which necessitates marked use of not only the long head, but also the medial and lateral heads of the triceps brachii.

The muscles of the front of the upper arm appear black because they do not contribute in the exercise.

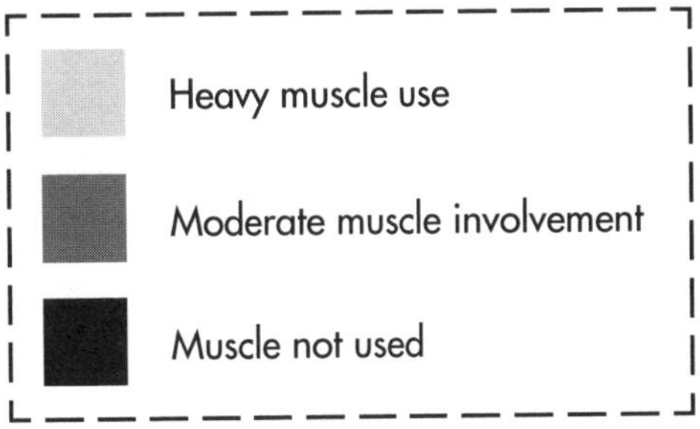

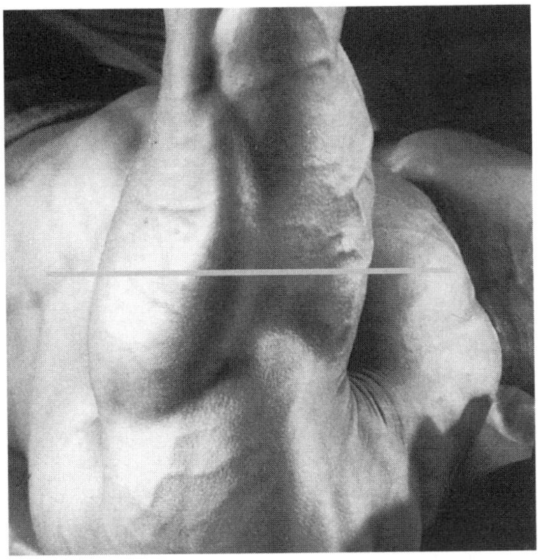

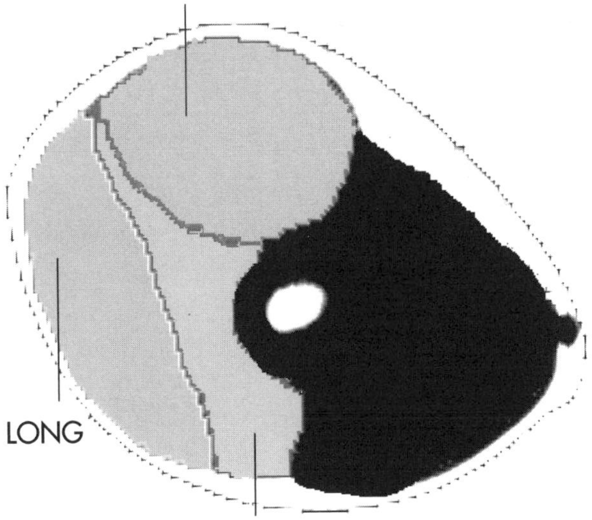

To understand the orientation of the MRI, raise your left arm beside your body, palm down, and imagine looking into a cross-sectional slice of it. The cross-section of the MRI is indicated by the bar in the photo.

3

SUPINE TRICEPS EXTENSION

With Dumbbell and Neutral Grip

A

TECHNIQUE

This is just like exercise 1, the French press with EZ bar and narrow grip, except you use dumbbells with palms facing each other. Lower the dumbbells as far as possible beside your head. Don't confuse this exercise with dumbbell flies or dumbbell bench press; keep the elbows stationary, held close together.

B

SUPINE TRICEPS EXTENSION

With Dumbbell and Neutral Grip

MUSCLE FUNCTION

The slight internal rotation of the palm—and the need to balance the weight with one arm—emphasizes stress of the lateral *head* of the triceps brachii. The medial and long heads are not left out; they show moderate use.

The muscles of the front of the upper arm appear black because they do not contribute in the exercise.

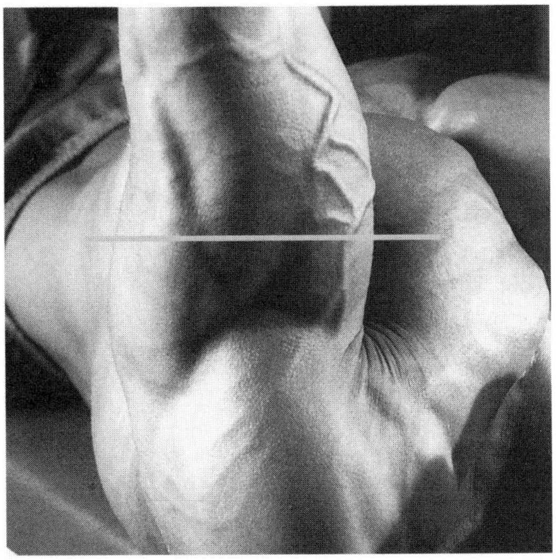

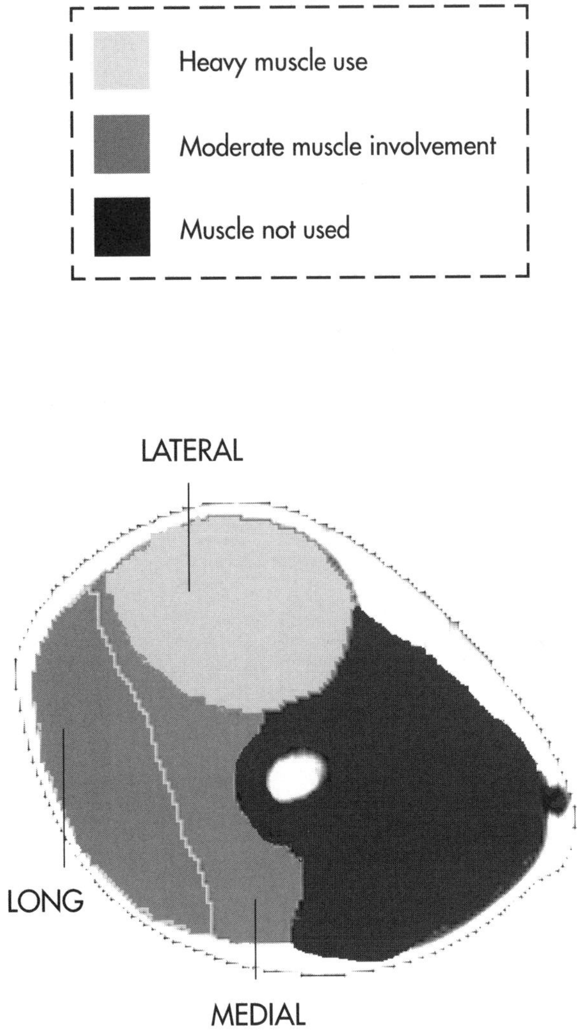

To understand the orientation of the MRI, raise your left arm beside your body, palm down, and imagine looking into a cross-sectional slice of it. The cross-section of the MRI is indicated by the bar in the photo.

4

OVERHEAD TRICEPS EXTENSION

With Dumbbell and Neutral Grip

A

TECHNIQUE

Raise dumbbell directly overhead until the arm is extended for the starting position. Using the neutral grip, lower dumbbell in smooth fashion behind the head as far as possible by flexing at the elbow. Pause, then raise the dumbbell to the starting position by contracting the elbow extensors. Remember, keep the upper arm vertical to the floor and directly beside the head. This is not a pressing exercise.

B

OVERHEAD TRICEPS EXTENSION

With Dumbbell and Neutral Grip

MUSCLE FUNCTION

This exercise allows a marked range of motion about the elbow joint, and a fair amount of weight can be used with the neutral grip. In this exercise, *all three heads* of the triceps brachii are markedly stressed.

The muscles of the front of the upper arm appear black because they do not contribute in the exercise.

Heavy muscle use
Moderate muscle involvement
Muscle not used

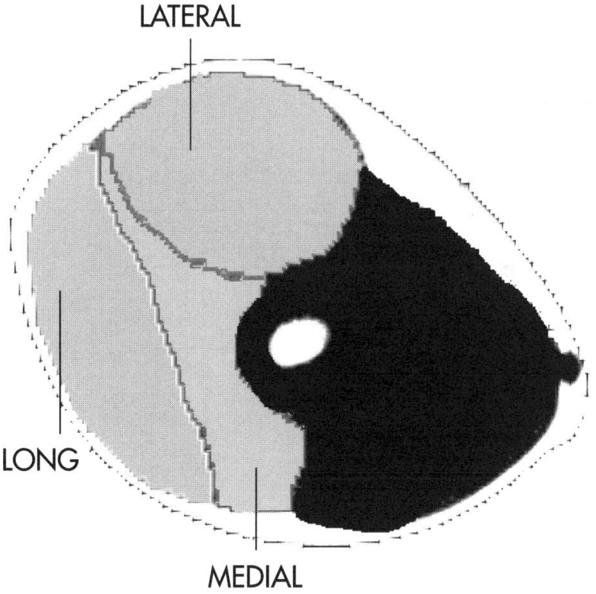

To understand the orientation of the MRI, raise your left arm beside your body, palm down, and imagine looking into a cross-sectional slice of it. The cross-section of the MRI is indicated by the bar in the photo.

5

OVERHEAD TRICEPS EXTENSION

With Dumbbell and Rotation

BACK OF UPPER ARM

A

B

TECHNIQUE

This is just like exercise 4, except that as the dumbbell passes by the head on the way up (when the elbow is at about 90 degrees) the hand is rotated out so that the palm faces away from the body at full arm extension. This is the starting position. With the palm facing away from the body, begin lowering the dumbbell smoothly by flexing at the elbow. As soon as movement starts, also begin to rotate the palm inward so that when the dumbbell passes the head (elbow at about 90 degrees), the hand is in the neutral position. Pause, then raise the dumbbell to the starting position by contracting the elbow extensors. As the dumbbell passes the head, rotate the palm away from the body. Remember, keep the upper arm vertical to the floor and directly beside the head. This is not a pressing exercise.

OVERHEAD TRICEPS EXTENSION

With Dumbbell and Rotation

MUSCLE FUNCTION

As you can see, this exercise takes a lot out of *all three heads* of the triceps brachii.

The muscles of the front of the upper arm appear black because they do not contribute in the exercise.

- Heavy muscle use
- Moderate muscle involvement
- Muscle not used

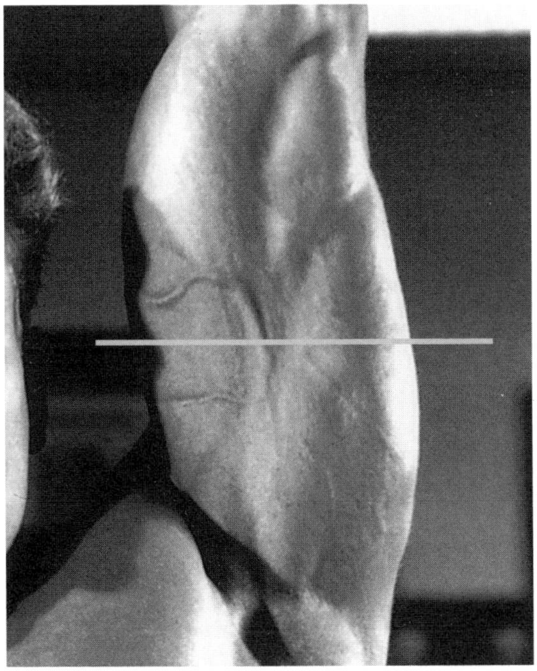

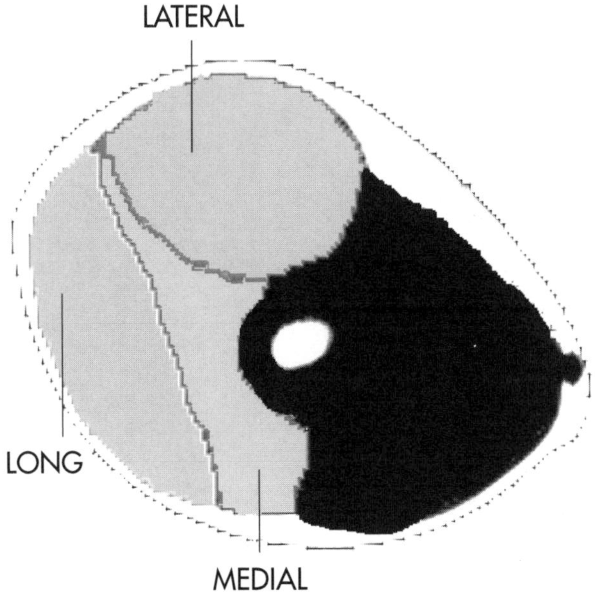

To understand the orientation of the MRI, raise your left arm beside your body, palm down, and imagine looking into a cross-sectional slice of it. The cross-section of the MRI is indicated by the bar in the photo.

6 OVERHEAD TRICEPS EXTENSION

With Reverse Grip

A

TECHNIQUE

Achieve starting position using a reverse grip on the dumbbell. Lean slightly to the side and put your hand on the bench for support. Keep the dumbbell horizontal to the floor throughout the movement, making sure the elbow is kept stationary and is extended at the starting position.

B

OVERHEAD TRICEPS EXTENSION

With Reverse Grip

MUSCLE FUNCTION

Oh, yeah, feel that stretch. This exercise also allows a decent range of motion about the elbow joint. The hand position, however, limits the amount of weight that can be used. Only the long head shows marked use. The medial and lateral heads of the triceps brachii provide moderate support.

The muscles of the front of the upper arm appear black because they do not contribute in the exercise.

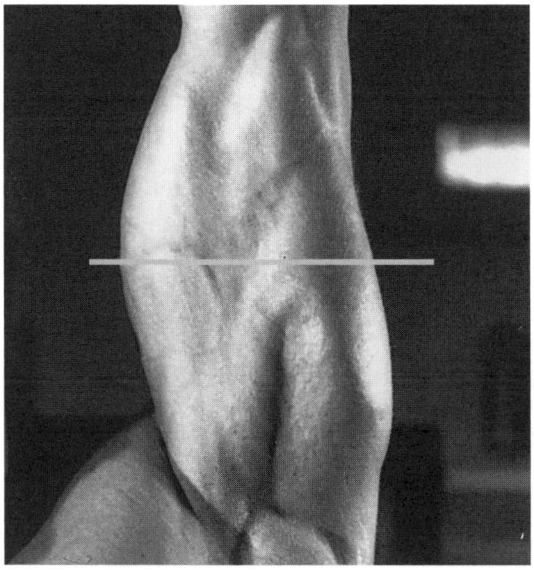

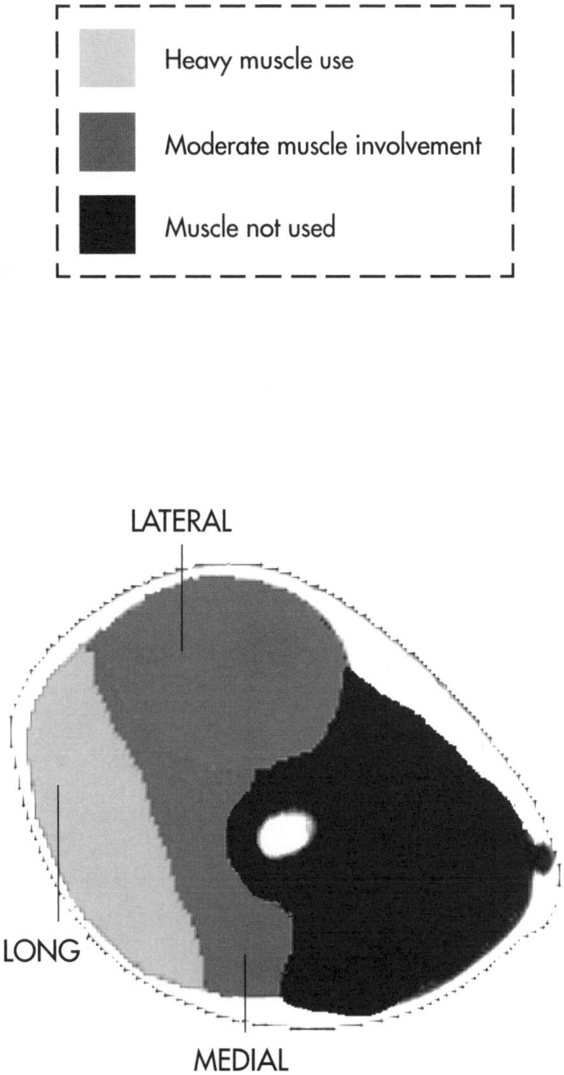

To understand the orientation of the MRI, raise your left arm beside your body, palm down, and imagine looking into a cross-sectional slice of it. The cross-section of the MRI is indicated by the bar in the photo.

7

BACK OF UPPER ARM

STANDING FRENCH PRESS

With Straight Bar

A

TECHNIQUE

The idea here is to keep the upper arms upright and parallel with the long axis of the body. The grip is shoulder width with the palms up. Raise the bar over your head by extending at the elbows. Extend until the bar is completely overhead, pause, and then lower the bar smoothly to the starting position.

B

STANDING FRENCH PRESS

With Straight Bar

MUSCLE FUNCTION

For this exercise, the medial and lateral heads of the triceps brachii do the majority of the work, with the long head providing some support.

The muscles of the front of the upper arm appear black because they do not contribute in the exercise.

Heavy muscle use

Moderate muscle involvement

Muscle not used

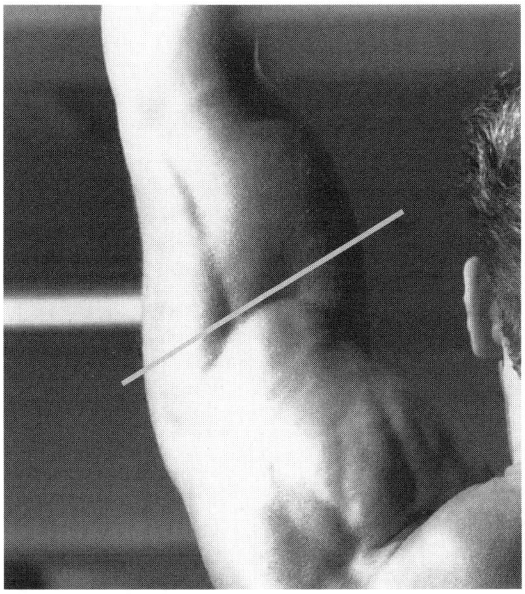

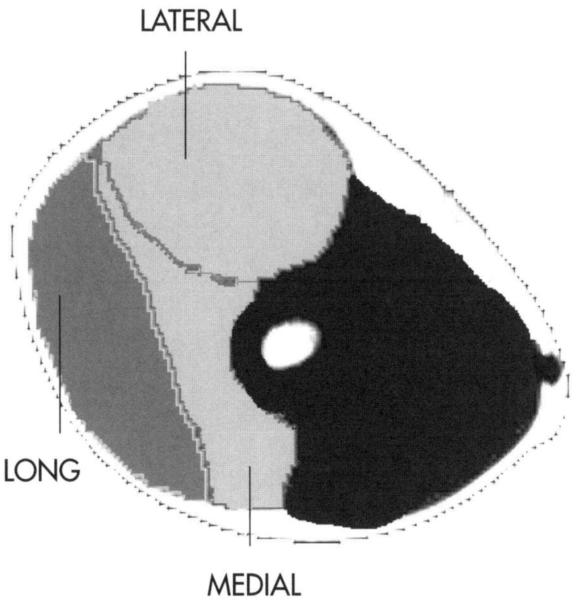

To understand the orientation of the MRI, raise your left arm beside your body, palm down, and imagine looking into a cross-sectional slice of it. The cross-section of the MRI is indicated by the bar in the photo.

8

TRICEPS PUSH DOWN

With Straight Bar and Narrow Grip

A

TECHNIQUE

This is a classic pulley machine exercise for developing the triceps. Start the exercise by contracting the triceps, pushing the bar down until your arms are straight. After a short pause, relax somewhat and the weight will raise the bar. Remember, control this motion. Let the weight raise the bar until the elbows are flexed well beyond 90 degrees, and you will be back to the starting position. It is important to keep your elbows close to your sides and immobile during the course of the exercise.

B

TRICEPS PUSH DOWN

With Straight Bar and Narrow Grip

MUSCLE FUNCTION

So you want the horseshoe. This is one that will do it. Both the long and lateral heads of the triceps brachii get the job done in this case. The medial head is not left out, providing moderate assistance.

The muscles of the front of the upper arm appear black because they do not contribute in the exercise.

Heavy muscle use

Moderate muscle involvement

Muscle not used

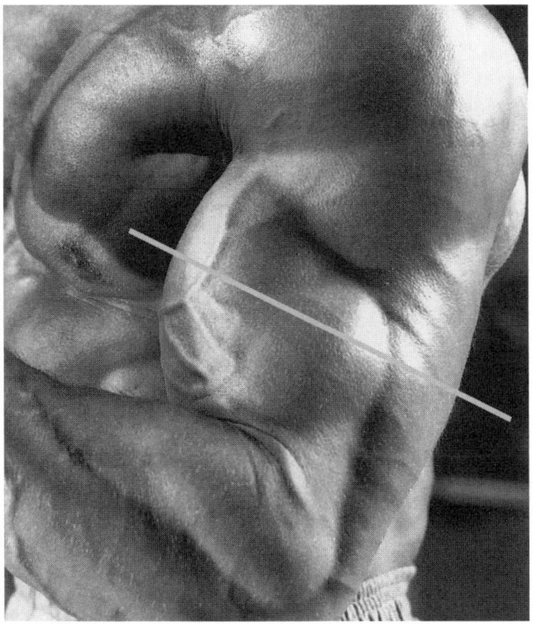

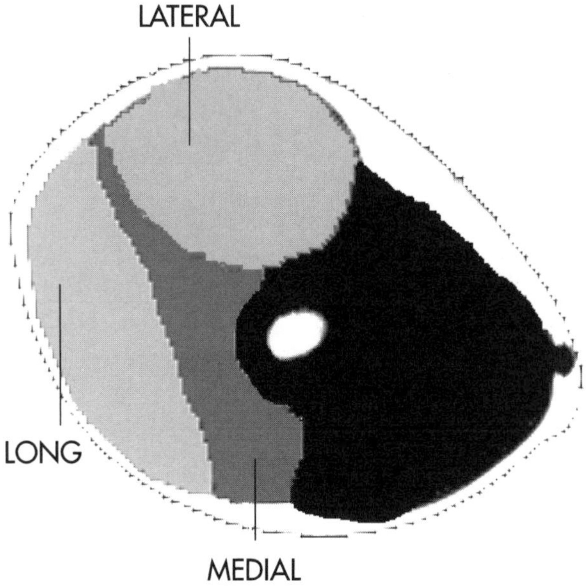

To understand the orientation of the MRI, raise your left arm beside your body, palm down, and imagine looking into a cross-sectional slice of it. The cross-section of the MRI is indicated by the bar in the photo.

9

TRICEPS PUSH DOWN

With Rope

BACK OF UPPER ARM

A

TECHNIQUE

This is very similar to exercise 8 except a rope is used, which allows two things: (1) the exercise is started at the top with the hands essentially in the neutral position, and (2) during the course of the push down, the wrists are rotated inward so that at complete elbow extension the palms are down. As the weight pulls the rope back up, the wrists are rotated so that at the top of the ascent the hands are again in the neutral position.

B

TRICEPS PUSH DOWN

With Rope

MUSCLE FUNCTION

As some have put forth, adding that little twist at the bottom is all it takes. Now, *all three heads* of the triceps brachii are getting taxed to the max.

The muscles of the front of the upper arm appear black because they do not contribute in the exercise.

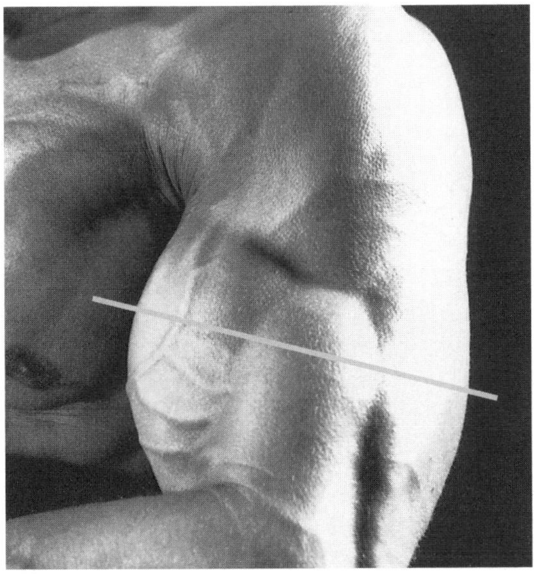

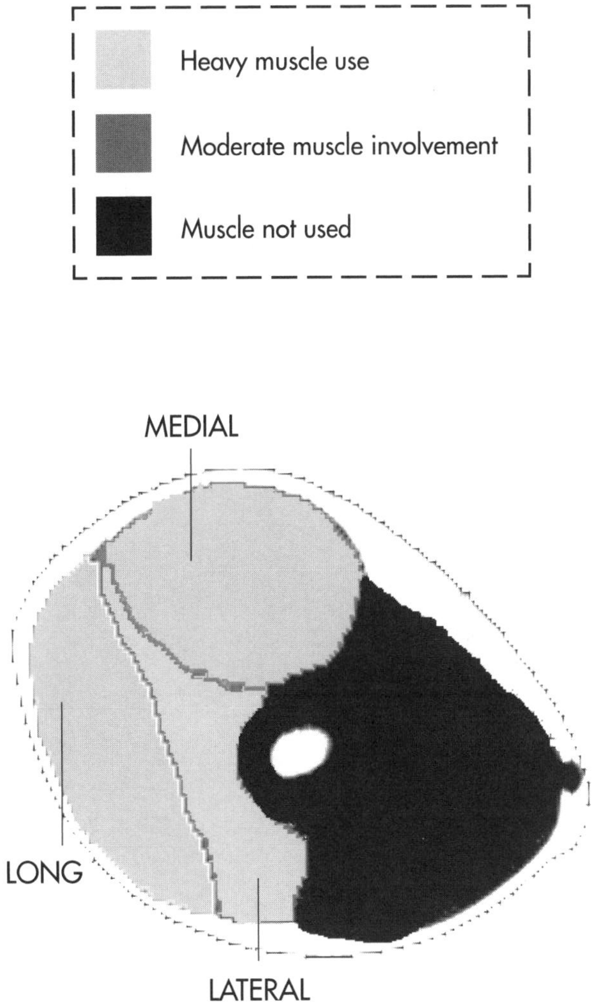

To understand the orientation of the MRI, raise your left arm beside your body, palm down, and imagine looking into a cross-sectional slice of it. The cross-section of the MRI is indicated by the bar in the photo.

10

TRICEPS PUSH DOWN

With Angled Bar

A

TECHNIQUE

This is just like exercise 9, except an angled bar is used to keep the grip just short of neutral.

B

TRICEPS PUSH DOWN

With Angled Bar

MUSCLE FUNCTION

Again, it seems that getting the hand to the neutral position is one way of taxing *all three heads* of the triceps brachii to the maximum.

The muscles of the front of the upper arm appear black because they do not contribute in the exercise.

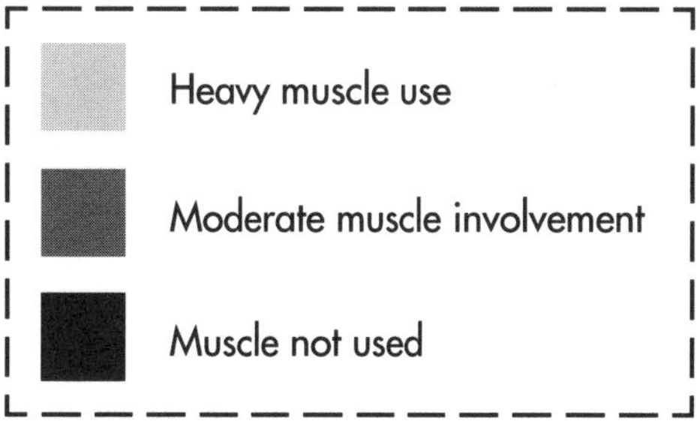

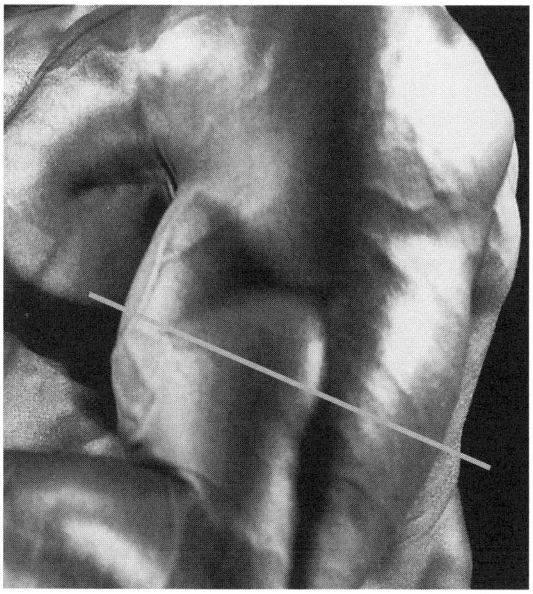

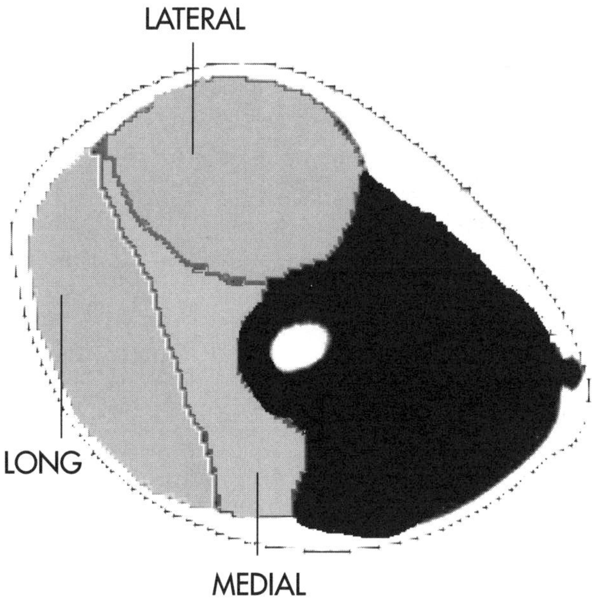

To understand the orientation of the MRI, raise your left arm beside your body, palm down, and imagine looking into a cross-sectional slice of it. The cross-section of the MRI is indicated by the bar in the photo.

11

ONE-ARM TRICEPS PUSH DOWN

A

TECHNIQUE

Start the exercise by extending the elbow joint, pushing the pulley machine's handle down until the arm is straight. After a short pause, relax somewhat and the weight will raise itself. Remember, control this motion. Let the weight raise the handle until the elbow is flexed beyond 90 degrees and you will be back to the starting position. It is important to keep the elbow immobile during the course of the exercise. Keep the torso still, the upper arm in close, and just use the triceps.

B

ONE-ARM TRICEPS PUSH DOWN

MUSCLE FUNCTION

As is obvious from the image, this exercise requires differential use of the three heads of the triceps brachii. The long head carries less of the load, while the medial and lateral heads take on the brunt of the work.

The muscles of the front of the upper arm appear black because they do not contribute in the exercise.

- Heavy muscle use
- Moderate muscle involvement
- Muscle not used

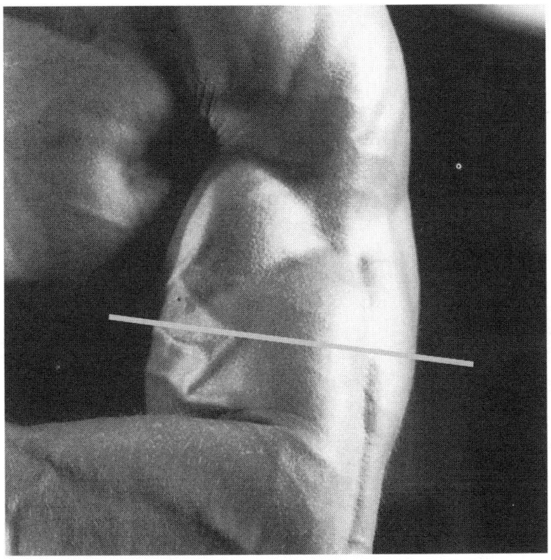

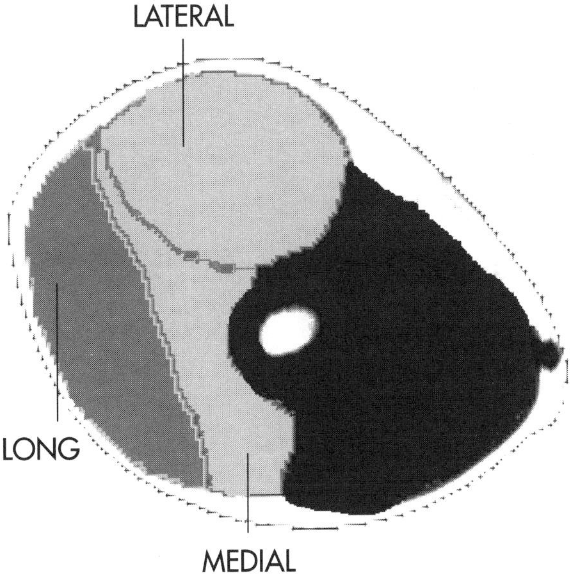

To understand the orientation of the MRI, raise your left arm beside your body, palm down, and imagine looking into a cross-sectional slice of it. The cross-section of the MRI is indicated by the bar in the photo.

12

ONE-ARM TRICEPS PUSH DOWN

With Reverse Grip

A

TECHNIQUE

This is just like exercise 11, except that a reverse grip is used on the handle.

B

ONE-ARM TRICEPS PUSH DOWN

With Reverse Grip

MUSCLE FUNCTION

Oh, do we feel weak. Even without a lot of weight, this exercise seems to markedly tax *all three heads* of the triceps brachii.

The muscles of the front of the upper arm appear black because they do not contribute in the exercise.

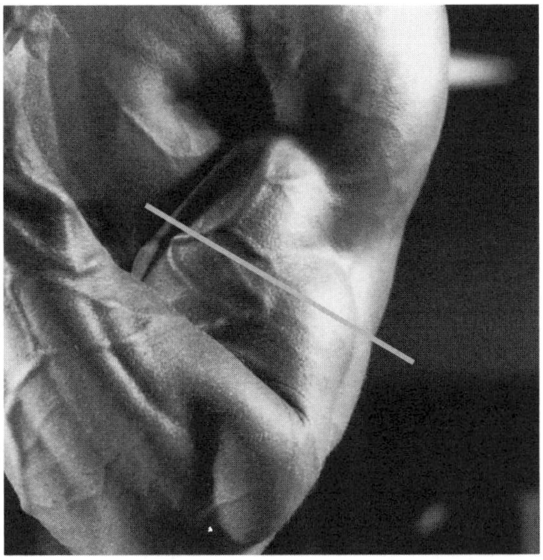

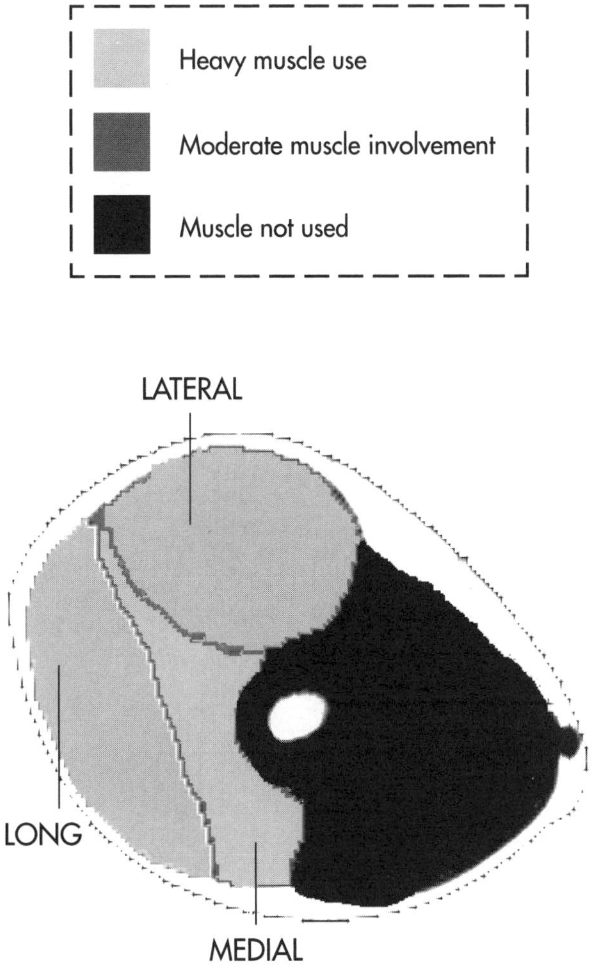

To understand the orientation of the MRI, raise your left arm beside your body, palm down, and imagine looking into a cross-sectional slice of it. The cross-section of the MRI is indicated by the bar in the photo.

13

OVERHEAD TRICEPS EXTENSION

With Rope

BACK OF UPPER ARM

A

TECHNIQUE

The most difficult part of this exercise may be getting into position to do it. During extension at the elbow joint, be sure and keep your upper arms stationary beside your head. Try to eliminate any extraneous body movement, and complete the movement until you reach full extension. After a short pause, relax, allowing the weight stack to descend; this pulls your hands far behind your head to the starting position.

B

OVERHEAD TRICEPS EXTENSION

With Rope

MUSCLE FUNCTION

If this exercise is difficult to do, the benefits should be worth it. This one really taxes the lateral head of the triceps brachii, while some help is provided by its neighbors, the medial and long heads.

The muscles of the front of the upper arm appear black because they do not contribute in the exercise.

Heavy muscle use
Moderate muscle involvement
Muscle not used

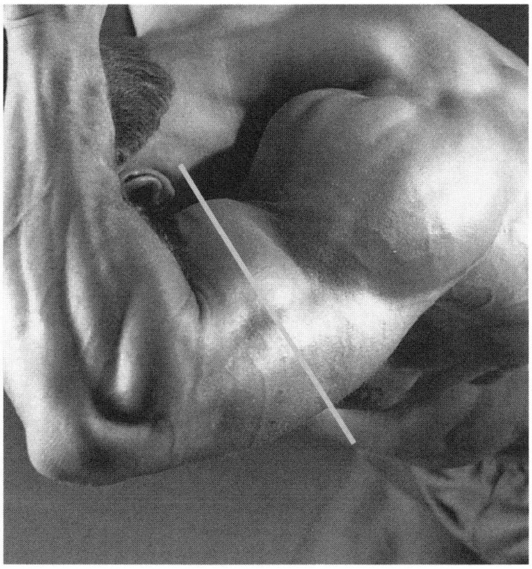

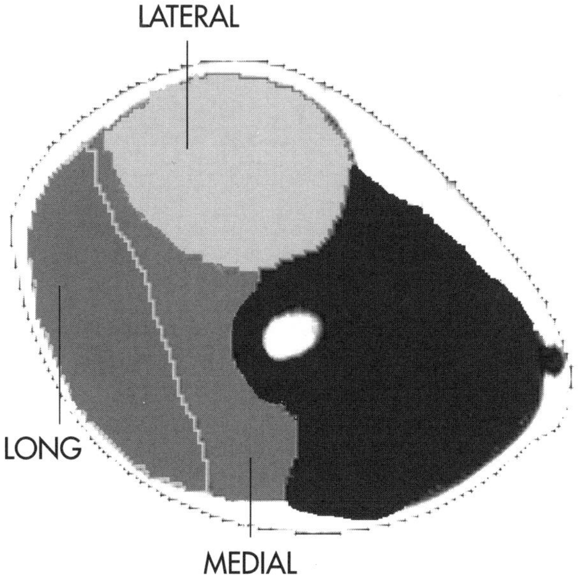

To understand the orientation of the MRI, raise your left arm beside your body, palm down, and imagine looking into a cross-sectional slice of it. The cross-section of the MRI is indicated by the bar in the photo.

14

BENCH PRESS

With Narrow Grip

A

TECHNIQUE

This is fairly self-explanatory. The lift is done palms up, with the thumbs under the bar. Smoothly lower the load to the chest, pause, then smoothly raise it to the straight-arm position. The idea here is not to crack the sternum, so do not bounce the weight. Hold your elbows close to your body throughout the range of motion. No bridging—keep your butt on the bench.

B

BENCH PRESS

With Narrow Grip

MUSCLE FUNCTION

The medial and lateral heads of the triceps brachii are really stressed in this exercise. The long head, in contrast, seems only moderately engaged.

The muscles of the front of the upper arm appear black because they do not contribute in the exercise.

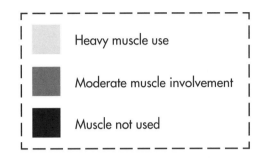

Heavy muscle use

Moderate muscle involvement

Muscle not used

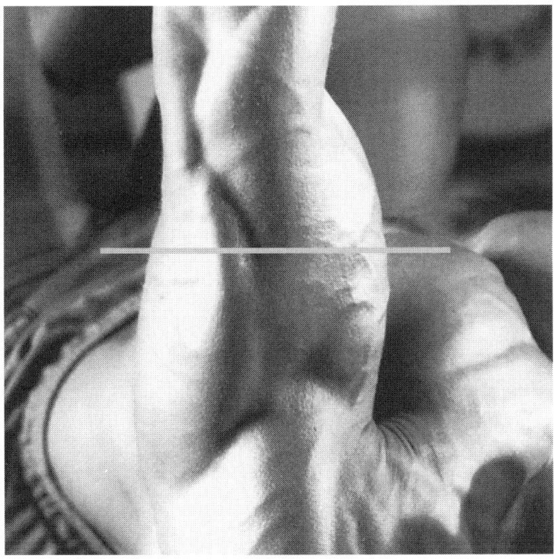

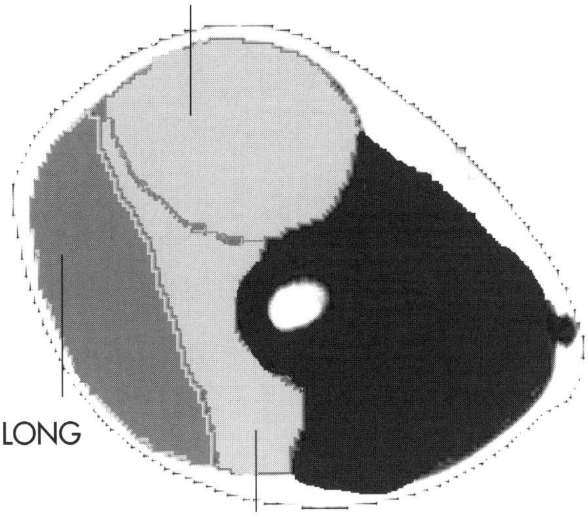

To understand the orientation of the MRI, raise your left arm beside your body, palm down, and imagine looking into a cross-sectional slice of it. The cross-section of the MRI is indicated by the bar in the photo.

15

PARALLEL BAR DIP

With Neutral Grip

BACK OF UPPER ARM

A

TECHNIQUE

This is another classic for triceps. Hop up in the dip bars to get started. Lower your body by relaxing somewhat. Keep your torso upright and descend as far as possible—at least until your elbows are past 90 degrees. Keep the elbows in tight. Pause at the bottom, and then push up, keeping your torso upright and your elbows in tight. Eliminate extraneous movement of your legs and head; just blast those triceps. If more stress is needed, hang a few plates on your belt.

B

PARALLEL BAR DIP

With Neutral Grip

MUSCLE FUNCTION

All three heads of the triceps brachii are markedly used as you raise and lower your body in the exercise that can really pump those triceps.

The muscles of the front of the upper arm appear black because they do not contribute in the exercise.

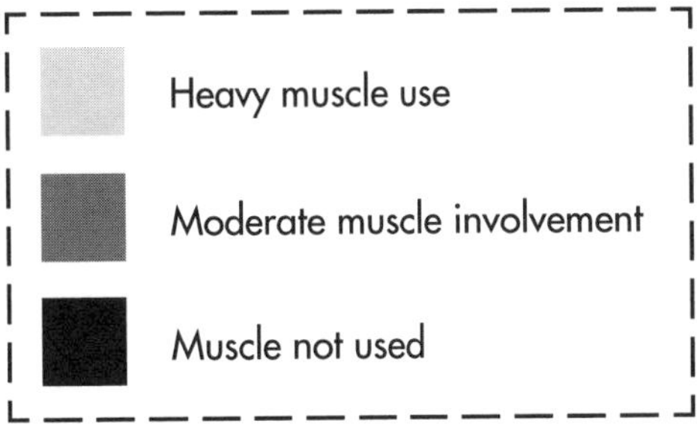

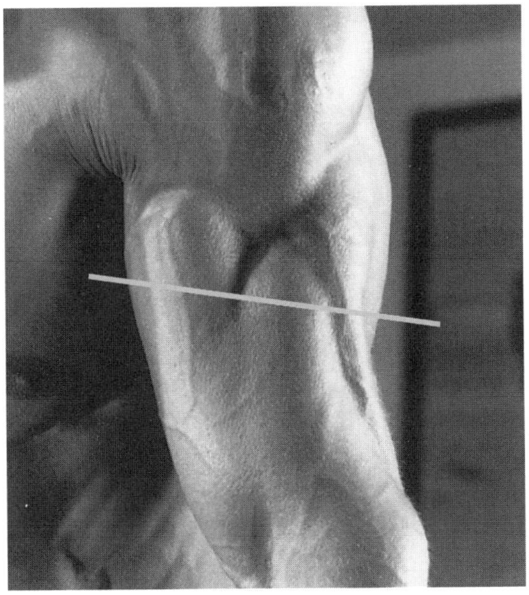

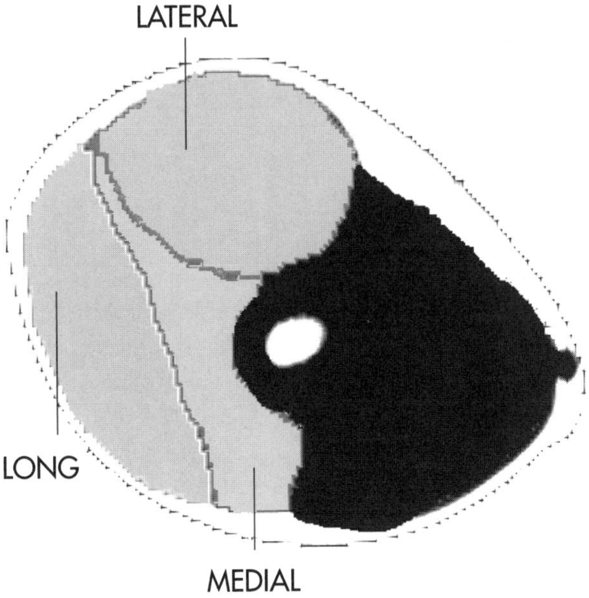

To understand the orientation of the MRI, raise your left arm beside your body, palm down, and imagine looking into a cross-sectional slice of it. The cross-section of the MRI is indicated by the bar in the photo.

16

BENCH DIP

A

TECHNIQUE

The most important thing here is to do this exercise with a lot of control. Keep the hands pointed toward the feet, the arms straight, and then lower yourself as far as possible. After a nice, smooth descent and a slight pause, use mainly elbow extension to raise yourself to the starting position.

B

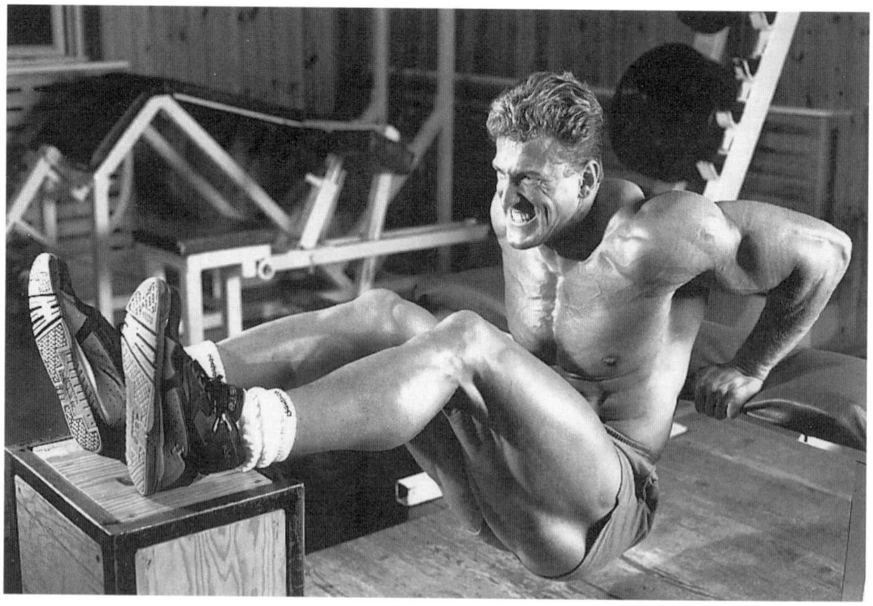

BENCH DIP

MUSCLE FUNCTION

The fact that *all heads* of the triceps brachii are markedly used in this exercise should not be overly surprising because dips between benches and between parallel bars are quite similar.

The muscles of the front of the upper arm appear black because they do not contribute in the exercise.

Heavy muscle use

Moderate muscle involvement

Muscle not used

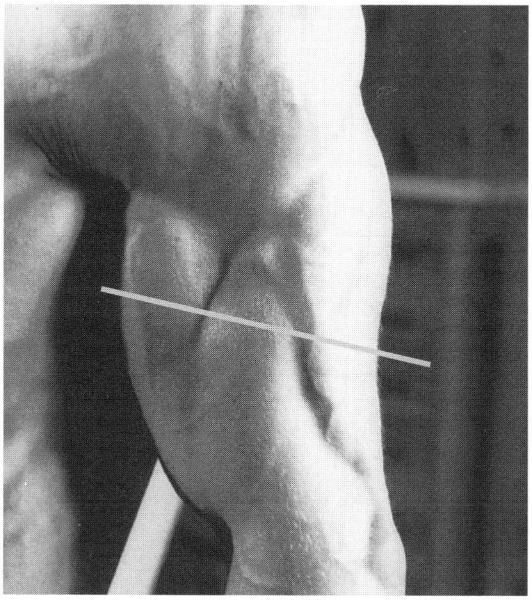

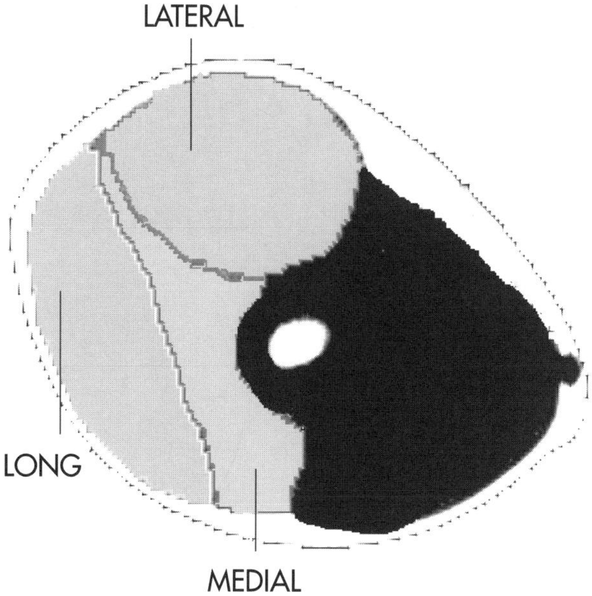

To understand the orientation of the MRI, raise your left arm beside your body, palm down, and imagine looking into a cross-sectional slice of it. The cross-section of the MRI is indicated by the bar in the photo.

17

PULLOVER

With EZ Bar and Narrow Grip

A

TECHNIQUE

Your head should be just off the end of the bench. Begin by lowering the weight so it is held slightly off the chest (not shown). Move the bar smoothly over the head, keeping it within an inch or so of the body. Now, lower the weight as far as possible toward the floor, keeping the elbows close together. Pause at the farthest stretch, then raise the bar to just off the chest. The next rep is started by again lowering the bar over the head. Keep your butt on the bench. This is not a pressing exercise; just clear the face on the way up and down.

B

PULLOVER

With EZ Bar and Narrow Grip

MUSCLE FUNCTION

The long head showed marked use compared to its counterparts, which were only slightly involved.

The muscles of the front of the upper arm appear black because they do not contribute in the exercise.

Heavy muscle use

Moderate muscle involvement

Muscle not used

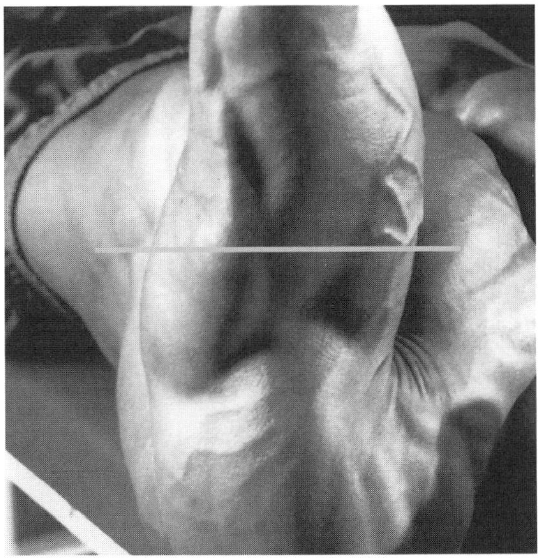

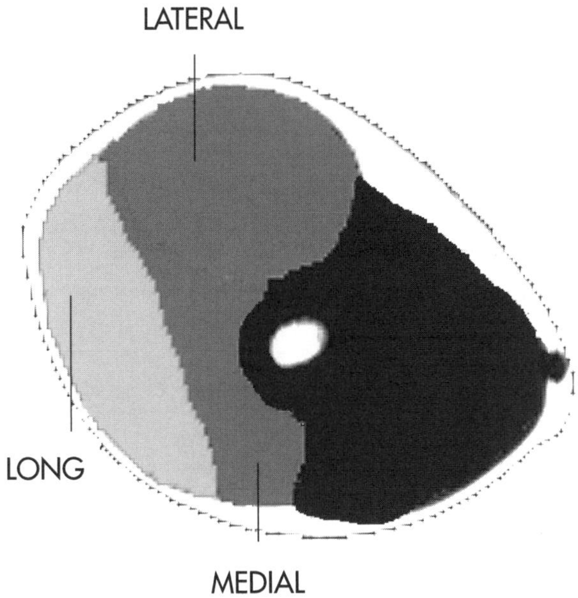

To understand the orientation of the MRI, raise your left arm beside your body, palm down, and imagine looking into a cross-sectional slice of it. The cross-section of the MRI is indicated by the bar in the photo.

18

KICK BACK

A

TECHNIQUE

The idea here is to really isolate the triceps. Keep the upper arm stationary, elbow tight to the body, and lower the weight till the elbow angle is 90 degrees. Keep the elbow stationary. Extend the elbow to raise the weight to the starting position.

B

KICK BACK

MUSCLE FUNCTION

In spite of the relatively light weight most of us use to do this exercise, it seems to require a lot from the triceps brachii, especially the medial and lateral heads.

The muscles of the front of the upper arm appear black because they do not contribute in the exercise.

(light)	Heavy muscle use
(medium)	Moderate muscle involvement
(black)	Muscle not used

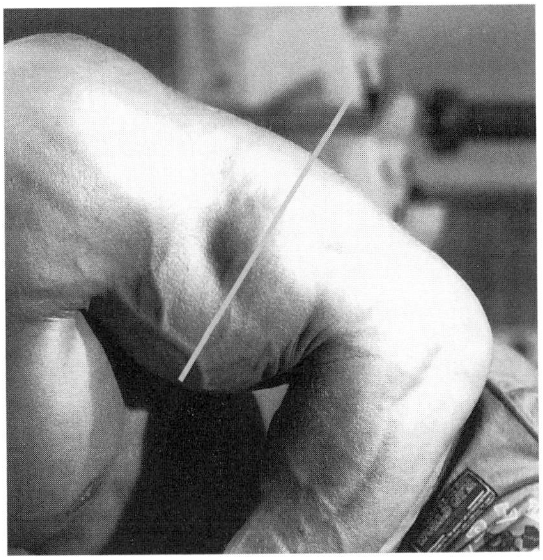

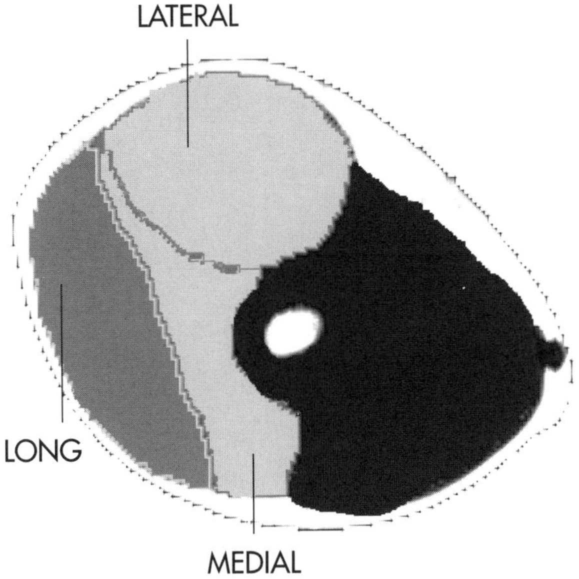

To understand the orientation of the MRI, raise your left arm beside your body, palm down, and imagine looking into a cross-sectional slice of it. The cross-section of the MRI is indicated by the bar in the photo.

19

MILITARY PRESS
With Straight Bar Behind Neck

A

TECHNIQUE

This is one of the most common exercises performed in the gym. Smoothly press the bar until your elbows are fully extended and the bar is directly overhead. Pause, and then lower the weight to the starting position.

B

MILITARY PRESS

With Straight Bar Behind Neck

MUSCLE FUNCTION

You may be surprised by these results. The *lateral* and *medial heads* of the triceps brachii seem to be critical for getting the bar overhead in this exercise, while the long head appears to provide no assistance.

The muscles of the front of the upper arm appear black because they do not contribute in the exercise.

Heavy muscle use

Moderate muscle involvement

Muscle not used

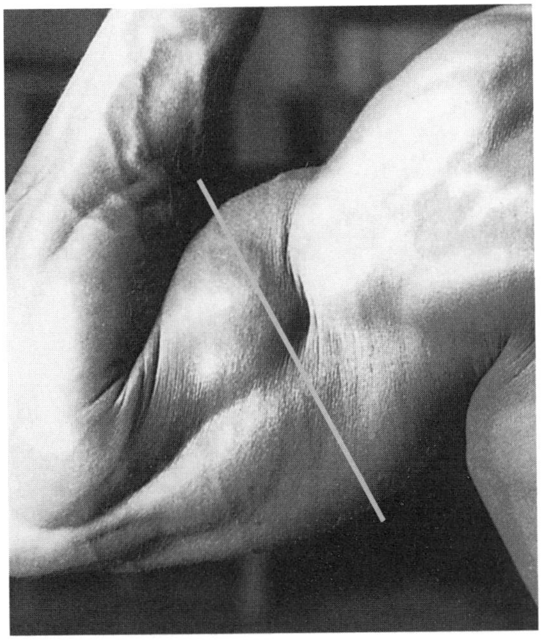

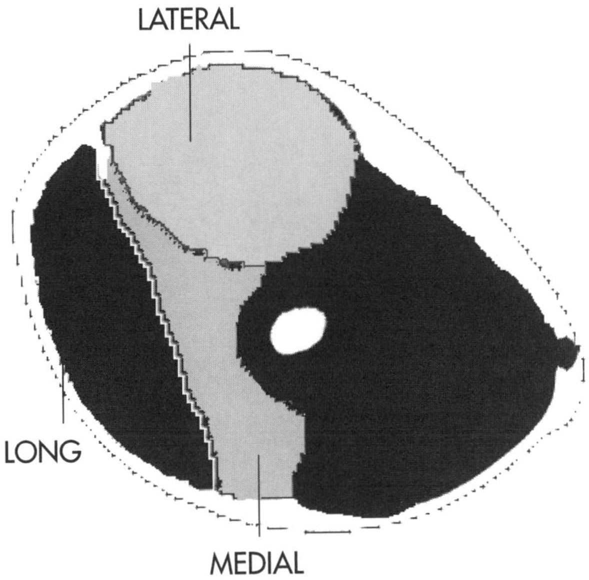

To understand the orientation of the MRI, raise your left arm beside your body, palm down, and imagine looking into a cross-sectional slice of it. The cross-section of the MRI is indicated by the bar in the photo.

20

STANDING DUMBBELL PRESS

With Elbows In

A

TECHNIQUE

Keeping the elbows in, press the dumbbells overhead. Once your elbows are extended, pause, and then smoothly lower the weight to the starting position. Try to keep your elbows in front of your body to emphasize the triceps, not the shoulders.

B

STANDING DUMBBELL PRESS

With Elbows In

MUSCLE FUNCTION

The pattern here is comparable to that of the military press; yet the involvement is less. The load for elbow extension is placed on the medial and lateral heads of the triceps brachii with the long head providing no help.

The muscles of the front of the upper arm appear black because they do not contribute in the exercise.

Heavy muscle use
Moderate muscle involvement
Muscle not used

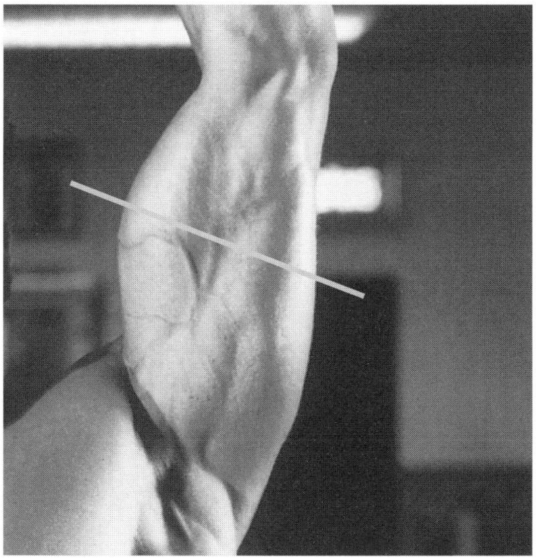

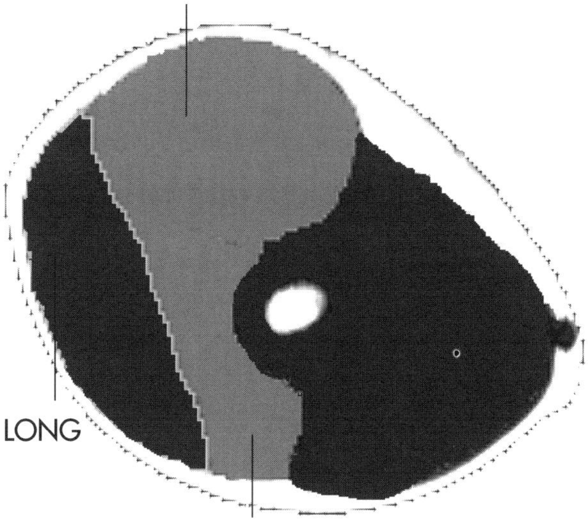

To understand the orientation of the MRI, raise your left arm beside your body, palm down, and imagine looking into a cross-sectional slice of it. The cross-section of the MRI is indicated by the bar in the photo.

MUSCLE USE GUIDE

Two Xs denote heavy muscle use; one X denotes moderate muscle involvement. No X is indicated for muscles that show no use during exercise.

		BACK OF THE UPPER ARM		
	EXERCISE NAME	LAT	LONG	MED
#1	**French Press** with EZ bar	X	XX	X
#2	**French Press** with EZ bar on decline bench	XX	XX	XX
#3	**Supine Triceps Extension** with dumbbell and neutral grip	XX	X	X
#4	**Overhead Triceps Extension** with dumbbell and neutral grip	XX	XX	XX
#5	**Overhead Triceps Extension** with dumbbell and rotation	XX	XX	XX
#6	**Overhead Triceps Extension** with reverse grip	X	XX	X
#7	**Standing French Press** with straight bar	XX	X	XX
#8	**Triceps Push Down** with straight bar and narrow grip	XX	XX	X
#9	**Triceps Push Down** with rope	XX	XX	XX
#10	**Triceps Push Down** with angled bar	XX	XX	XX
#11	**One-Arm Triceps Push Down**	XX	X	XX
#12	**One-Arm Triceps Push Down** with reverse grip	XX	XX	XX

	EXERCISE NAME	LAT	LONG	MED
#13	**Overhead Triceps Extension** with rope	XX	X	X
#14	**Bench Press** with narrow grip	XX	X	XX
#15	**Parallel Bar Dip** with neutral grip	XX	XX	XX
#16	**Bench Dip**	XX	XX	XX
#17	**Pullover** with EZ bar and narrow grip	X	XX	X
#18	**Kick Back**	XX	X	XX
#19	**Military Press** with straight bar behind neck	XX		XX
#20	**Standing Dumbbell Press** with elbows in	X		X

CHAPTER 4

THIGH

THE THIGH EXERCISES INVOLVE THREE MAJOR MUSCLE GROUPS: the knee extensors, the knee flexors, and the adductor muscles. Several exercises show heavy use of the three vasti muscles both in one-joint (i.e., the knee extension in exercise 2) and two-joint exercises (i.e., most squat exercises and the leg press). The rectus femoris appears to show heavy use only in exercises where movement is restricted to the knee joint (e.g., exercises 1-3 and 12). The adductor brevis and magnus muscles show heavy use in several knee extension exercises, including the hack squat and the leg press, where marked movement about the hip joint also occurs (e.g., exercises 9, 10, 13, and 14). Also, notice the modest use of m. biceps femoris and the hamstring muscles in the stiff-legged deadlift (exercises 15 and 16) and the two leg curl exercises (17 and 18). The chart at the end of the chapter will help you select the exercises that target the muscles of the thigh you want to develop.

7

THIGH

LUNGE

A

TECHNIQUE

This exercise takes coordination to perform, and most people have a tendency to do it incorrectly. The idea is to keep the torso erect. Step forward with the left leg two to three feet, allowing the body to descend toward the floor in a controlled way. Stop the descent when the knee of the right leg is about to touch the floor. The left knee should be flexed a little past 90 degrees. Now, using the left leg, drive up and step back to the starting position. You can alternate legs, or do unilateral lunges. Alternatively, instead of a bar, you can use a pair of dumbbells to perform this exercise.

B

LUNGE

MUSCLE FUNCTION

This exercise really hits the adductor magnus (AD M) and brevis (AD B) of the forward leg. It also involves the three vasti muscles (VL, VM, and VI), but moderately.

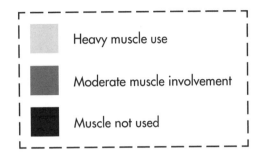

(light)	Heavy muscle use
(medium)	Moderate muscle involvement
(dark)	Muscle not used

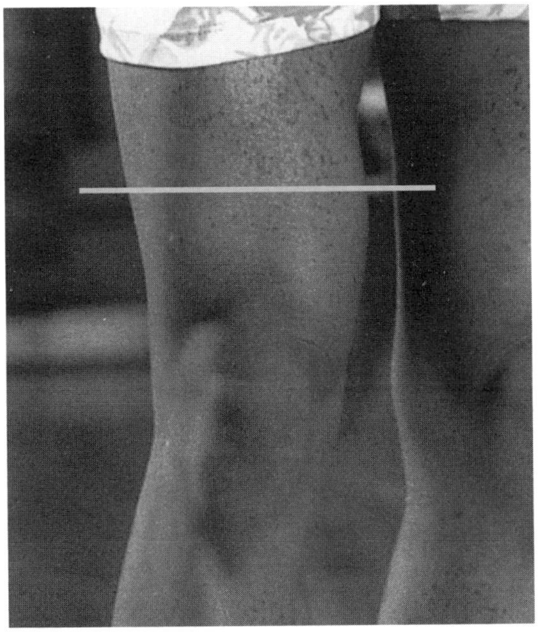

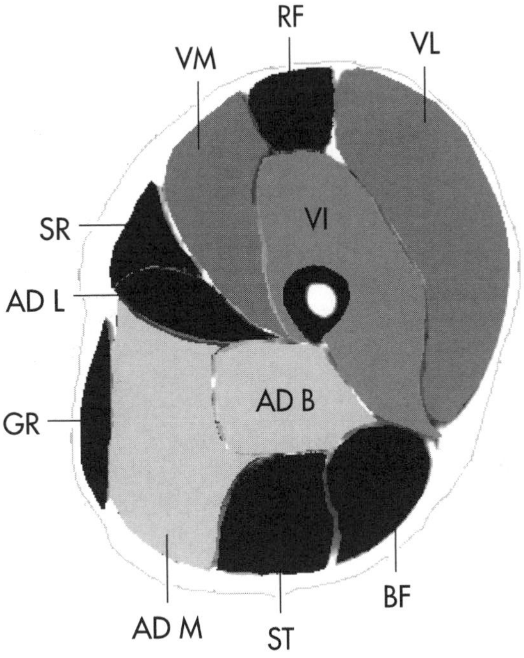

To understand the orientation of the MRI, stand and look down at your right leg and imagine looking into a cross-sectional slice of your right thigh. The cross-section of the MRI is indicated by the bar in the photo.

AD B = Adductor brevis
AD L = Adductor longus
AD M = Adductor magnus
BF = Biceps femoris
GR = Gracilis
RF = Rectus femoris
SR = Sartorius
ST = Semitendinosus
VM = Vastus medialis
VL = Vastus lateralis
VI = Vastus intermedius

2

SEATED KNEE EXTENSION

A

TECHNIQUE

The way to do this activity is self-explanatory. You can perform it as a unilateral or bilateral exercise. Raise the weight smoothly by contracting the thighs until the legs are completely extended, and after a slight pause, lower the load to the starting position. No cheating—keep your butt on the seat and sit still throughout the full range of motion.

B

SEATED KNEE EXTENSION

MUSCLE FUNCTION

This exercise activates all four muscles of the quadriceps femoris (VI, VM, VL, and RF) maximally. With the feet in a neutral position, the four muscles share the load equally.

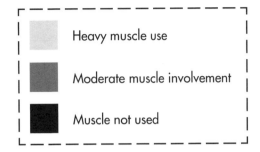

- Heavy muscle use
- Moderate muscle involvement
- Muscle not used

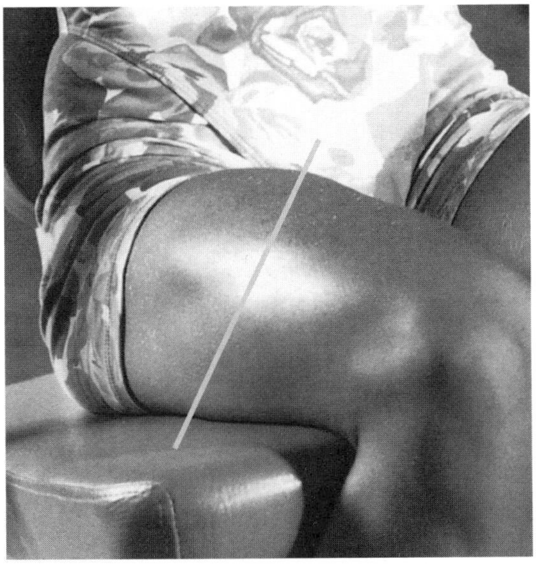

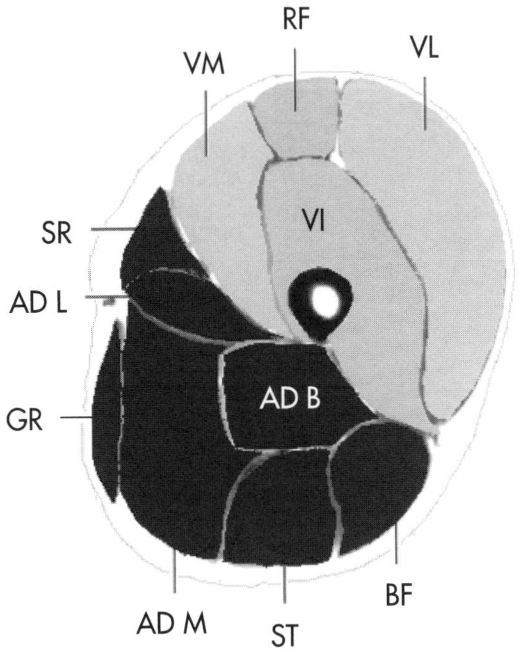

To understand the orientation of the MRI, stand and look down at your right leg and imagine looking into a cross-sectional slice of your right thigh. The cross-section of the MRI is indicated by the bar in the photo.

AD B	=	Adductor brevis
AD L	=	Adductor longus
AD M	=	Adductor magnus
BF	=	Biceps femoris
GR	=	Gracilis
RF	=	Rectus femoris
SR	=	Sartorius
ST	=	Semitendinosus
VM	=	Vastus medialis
VL	=	Vastus lateralis
VI	=	Vastus intermedius

3

SEATED KNEE EXTENSION

With Toes In

A

TECHNIQUE

This exercise is just like the last seated knee extension (exercise 2) except that the feet are rotated inward as far as possible throughout the full range of motion.

B

SEATED KNEE EXTENSION

With Toes In

MUSCLE FUNCTION

With the feet rotated inward, the rectus femoris (RF) and the vastus medialis(VM) show only moderate involvement, while the vastus lateralis (VL) and vastus intermedius (VI) are maximally stressed.

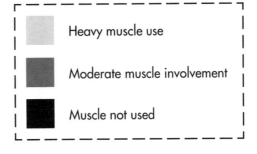

Heavy muscle use

Moderate muscle involvement

Muscle not used

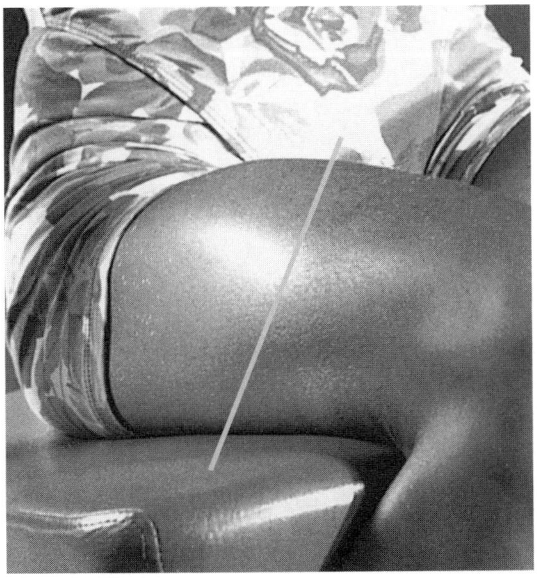

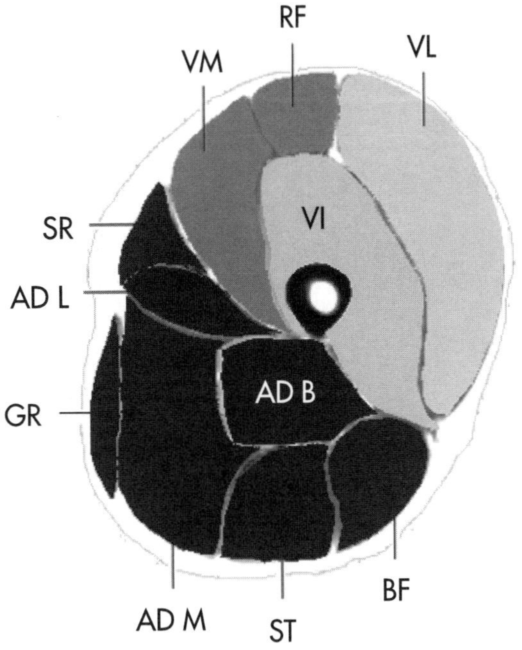

To understand the orientation of the MRI, stand and look down at your right leg and imagine looking into a cross-sectional slice of your right thigh. The cross-section of the MRI is indicated by the bar in the photo.

AD B	=	Adductor brevis
AD L	=	Adductor longus
AD M	=	Adductor magnus
BF	=	Biceps femoris
GR	=	Gracilis
RF	=	Rectus femoris
SR	=	Sartorius
ST	=	Semitendinosus
VM	=	Vastus medialis
VL	=	Vastus lateralis
VI	=	Vastus intermedius

4

SEATED KNEE EXTENSION

With Toes Out

A

TECHNIQUE

This is just like the last two seated knee extension exercises (exercises 2 and 3) except that the feet are rotated laterally as far as possible throughout the full range of motion.

B

SEATED KNEE EXTENSION

With Toes Out

MUSCLE FUNCTION

Rotation of the feet outward reduces involvement of the vastus lateralis (VL). The vastus medialis (VM), vastus intermedius (VI) and rectus femoris (RF) show maximal involvement.

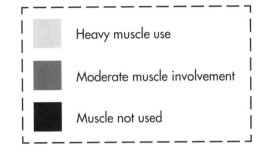

(light)	Heavy muscle use
(medium)	Moderate muscle involvement
(dark)	Muscle not used

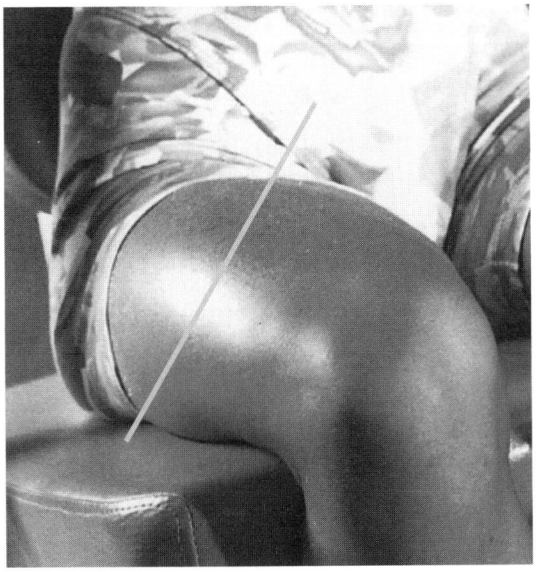

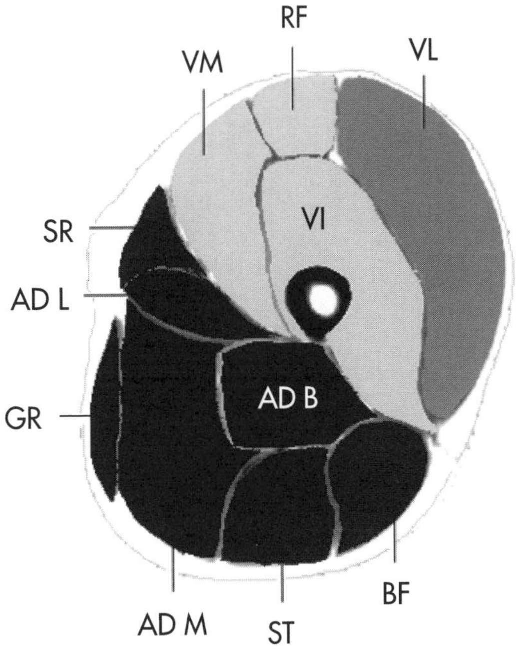

To understand the orientation of the MRI, stand and look down at your right leg and imagine looking into a cross-sectional slice of your right thigh. The cross-section of the MRI is indicated by the bar in the photo.

AD B = Adductor brevis
AD L = Adductor longus
AD M = Adductor magnus
BF = Biceps femoris
GR = Gracilis
RF = Rectus femoris
SR = Sartorius
ST = Semitendinosus
VM = Vastus medialis
VL = Vastus lateralis
VI = Vastus intermedius

5

THIGH

BACK SQUAT
With Narrow Stance

A

TECHNIQUE

Now we get down to some real exercise. Turn those legs to jelly, squat till you drop. Descend by driving the knees forward out over the toes and dropping the rump slightly behind the heels. Keep that back upright with a slight arch. Stop the descent when the thighs are about parallel to the floor. Now, keeping the torso upright, raise the bar in exactly the reverse motion of how it was lowered. Do not descend too fast, as stopping the bar at the bottom and raising it may require excessive forward lean. Remain upright to emphasize use of the thighs.

B

BACK SQUAT

With Narrow Stance

MUSCLE FUNCTION

This exercise stresses the three vasti muscles (VL, VI, and VM). The rectus femoris (RF), like the three adductor muscles (AD M, AD B, and AD L), shows moderate involvement. This is a good example illustrating that even some of the toughest quad exercises do not automatically stress all four heads.

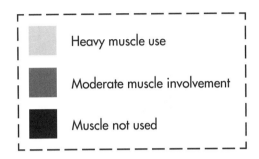

- Heavy muscle use
- Moderate muscle involvement
- Muscle not used

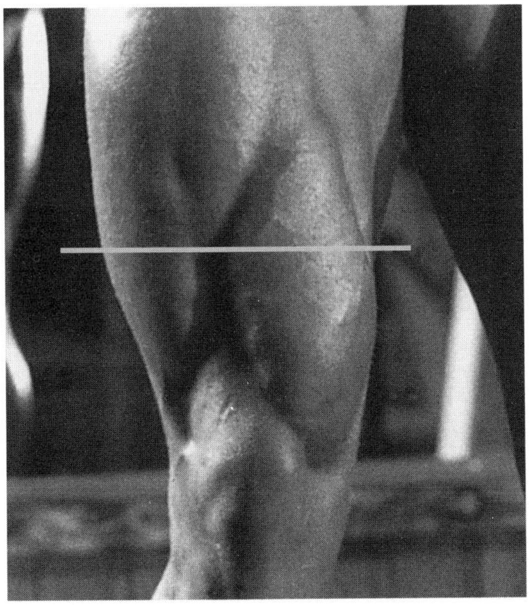

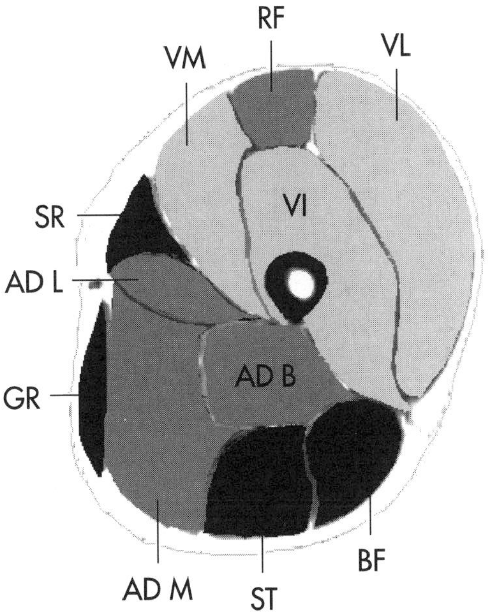

To understand the orientation of the MRI, stand and look down at your right leg and imagine looking into a cross-sectional slice of your right thigh. The cross-section of the MRI is indicated by the bar in the photo.

AD B = Adductor brevis
AD L = Adductor longus
AD M = Adductor magnus
BF = Biceps femoris
GR = Gracilis
RF = Rectus femoris
SR = Sartorius
ST = Semitendinosus
VM = Vastus medialis
VL = Vastus lateralis
VI = Vastus intermedius

6

CLASSICAL BACK SQUAT

A

TECHNIQUE

This is just like the narrow stance squat (exercise 5) except for position of the feet. This exercise should be done with toes pointed straight ahead or slightly out and the feet about shoulder width apart. So just hang some plates and do it.

B

CLASSICAL BACK SQUAT

MUSCLE FUNCTION

This exercise involves the three vasti muscles (VL, VM, and VI) most heavily. The rectus femoris (RF) and the three adductor muscles (AD M, AD L, and AD B) show moderate use. Why can you do more weight with this exercise? With this classical squat, as compared to the narrow stance squat, use of the powerful glutes and back muscles is probably greater. For isolation of the quads and additional use of the adductors, the narrow stance may be preferable.

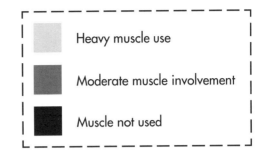

(light)	Heavy muscle use
(medium)	Moderate muscle involvement
(dark)	Muscle not used

AD B	=	Adductor brevis
AD L	=	Adductor longus
AD M	=	Adductor magnus
BF	=	Biceps femoris
GR	=	Gracilis
RF	=	Rectus femoris
SR	=	Sartorius
ST	=	Semitendinosus
VM	=	Vastus medialis
VL	=	Vastus lateralis
VI	=	Vastus intermedius

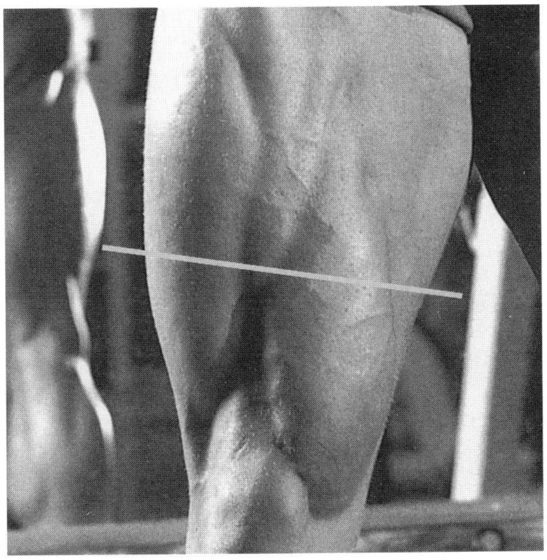

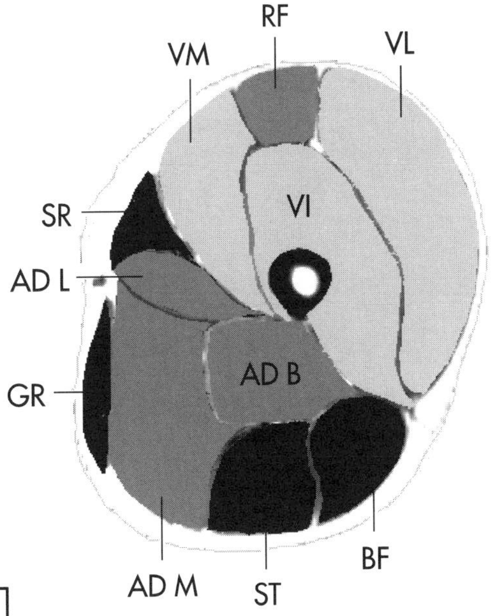

To understand the orientation of the MRI, stand and look down at your right leg and imagine looking into a cross-sectional slice of your right thigh. The cross-section of the MRI is indicated by the bar in the photo.

7

FRONT SQUAT

A

TECHNIQUE

This exercise is just like the classical squat (exercise 6) except that you are now holding the bar in front of your body. Place your feet about shoulder width apart with the toes pointed ahead or slightly out. Lower yourself nice and slowly until the thighs are parallel to the floor. Remember, keep your head up and back straight. Make a distinct stop and then push back up with good form.

B

FRONT SQUAT

MUSCLE FUNCTION

The front squat with barbell requires the same muscle use as the two back squat exercises (5 and 6). The three heads of the vasti muscle (VL, VI, and VM) are heavily used. The rectus femoris (RF) and the three adductor muscles (AD B, AD M, and AD B) show moderate stress.

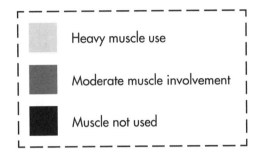

Heavy muscle use

Moderate muscle involvement

Muscle not used

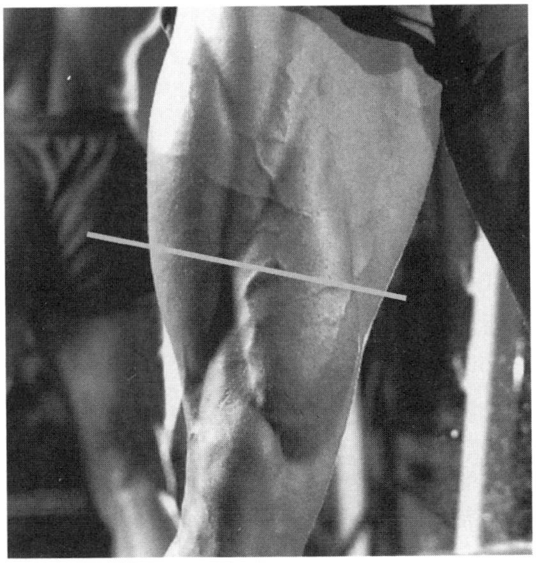

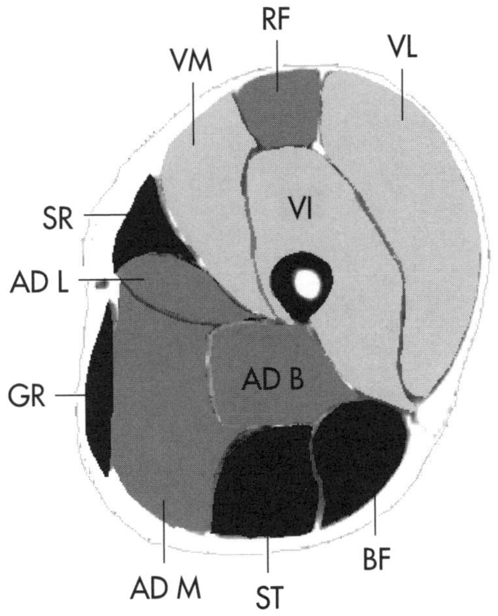

To understand the orientation of the MRI, stand and look down at your right leg and imagine looking into a cross-sectional slice of your right thigh. The cross-section of the MRI is indicated by the bar in the photo.

AD B = Adductor brevis
AD L = Adductor longus
AD M = Adductor magnus
BF = Biceps femoris
GR = Gracilis
RF = Rectus femoris
SR = Sartorius
ST = Semitendinosus
VM = Vastus medialis
VL = Vastus lateralis
VI = Vastus intermedius

8

FRONT SQUAT

in Smith Rack

A

TECHNIQUE

This is just like the last exercise (7) except that it is done in a Smith rack. Remember to keep the torso as erect as possible during this or any other squat. Squatting in front of a mirror always helps in maintaining good form.

B

FRONT SQUAT

in Smith Rack

MUSCLE FUNCTION

This exercise targets the three vasti muscles (VL, VM, and VI). The adductor magnus (AD M) and longus (AD L) are not used. There is moderate use of the rectus femoris (RF), sartorius (SR), semitendinosus (ST), adductor brevis (AD B) and biceps femoris (BF). This different pattern of muscle use from front squats may stem from the fact that the Smith machine makes it easier to maintain vertical movement.

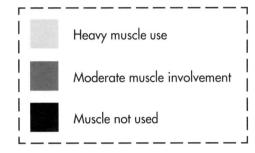

(light)	Heavy muscle use
(medium)	Moderate muscle involvement
(black)	Muscle not used

AD B	=	Adductor brevis
AD L	=	Adductor longus
AD M	=	Adductor magnus
BF	=	Biceps femoris
GR	=	Gracilis
RF	=	Rectus femoris
SR	=	Sartorius
ST	=	Semitendinosus
VM	=	Vastus medialis
VL	=	Vastus lateralis
VI	=	Vastus intermedius

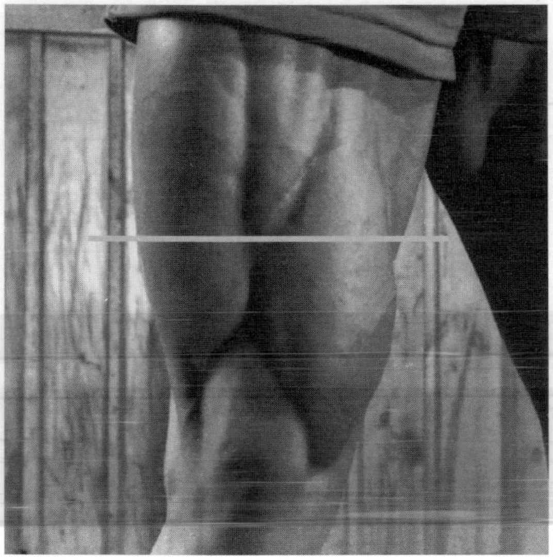

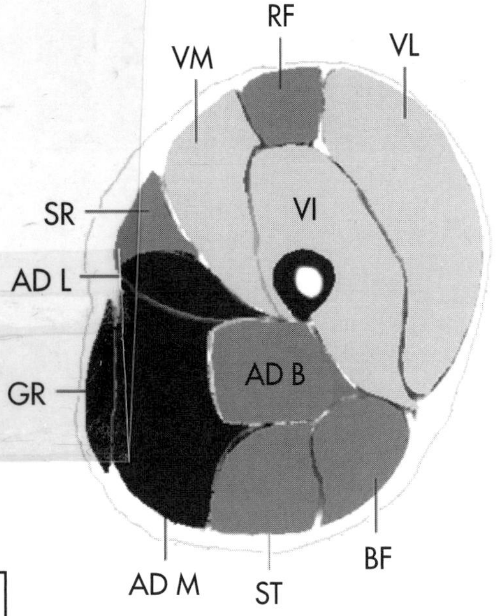

To understand the orientation of the MRI, stand and look down at your right leg and imagine looking into a cross-sectional slice of your right thigh. The cross-section of the MRI is indicated by the bar in the photo.

9

HACK SQUAT

With Feet in Front of Body

A

TECHNIQUE

So now you really want to isolate those quads. Hack squats are very comparable to free weight squats except for a few important items. In the hack squat, done in a machine, you do not have to balance a bar—just push against the resistance through your shoulders. Also the feet are placed on a special platform. This gives you the opportunity to place the base of support, your feet, directly under your hips, or as done in this version of the hack squat, out in front of your body. Hack squats also allow for a more complete range of motion, as descent is usually not stopped until the knee joint is flexed well beyond 90 degrees. Finally, the load is placed upon the body by slightly extending at the hip and knee joints (this raises the sledge) and moving the mechanical stops so you can lower the weight. Good luck, and just bust some reps!

B

HACK SQUAT

With Feet in Front of Body

MUSCLE FUNCTION

This exercise involves some muscles that we have not seen activated in previous squat exercises. The vastus lateralis (VL) and intermedius (VI) do the majority of the work, along with the large adductor magnus (AD M) and brevis (AD B). The vastus medialis (VM), gracilis (GR) and sartorius (SR) muscles are moderately used. The rectus femoris (RF) is not used.

Heavy muscle use

Moderate muscle involvement

Muscle not used

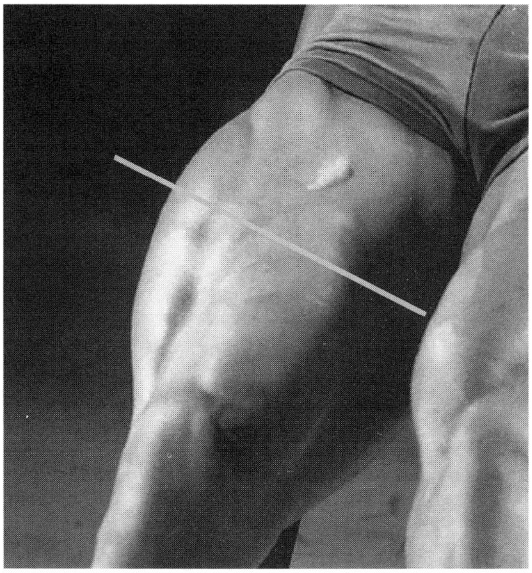

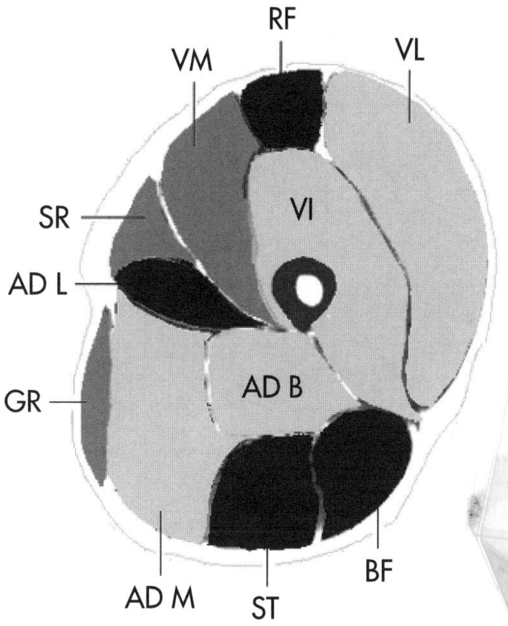

To understand the orientation of the MRI, stand and look down at your right leg and imagine looking into a cross-sectional slice of your right thigh. The cross-section of the MRI is indicated by the bar in the photo.

AD B	=	Adductor brevis
AD L	=	Adductor longus
AD M	=	Adductor magnus
BF	=	Biceps femoris
GR	=	Gracilis
RF	=	Rectus femoris
SR	=	Sartorius
ST	=	Semitendinosus
VM	=	Vastus medialis
VL	=	Vastus lateralis
VI	=	Vastus intermedius

10

HACK SQUAT
With Feet Under Hips

A

TECHNIQUE

This is just like exercise 9 except the feet are placed directly under the hips.

B

HACK SQUAT

With Feet Under Hips

MUSCLE FUNCTION

Placing the feet under the hips evokes even greater muscle use than the previous hack squat exercise. The vastus lateralis (VL) and intermedius (VI) and the adductor magnus (AD M) and brevis (AD B) muscles, as well as the gracilis (GR), show maximal stress. The rectus femoris, vastus medialis, sartorius, and adductor longus are also quite involved.

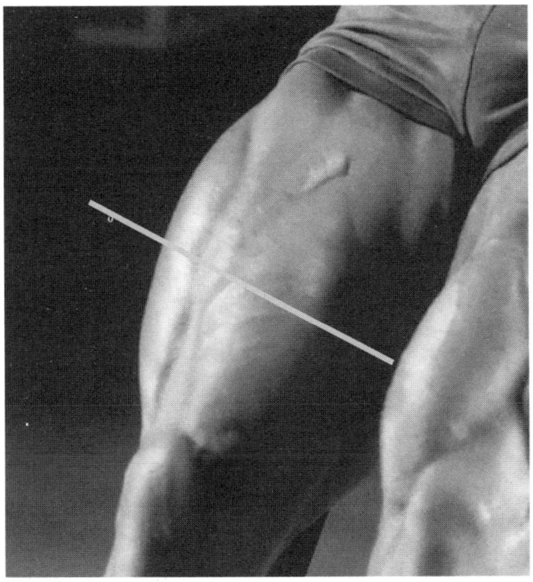

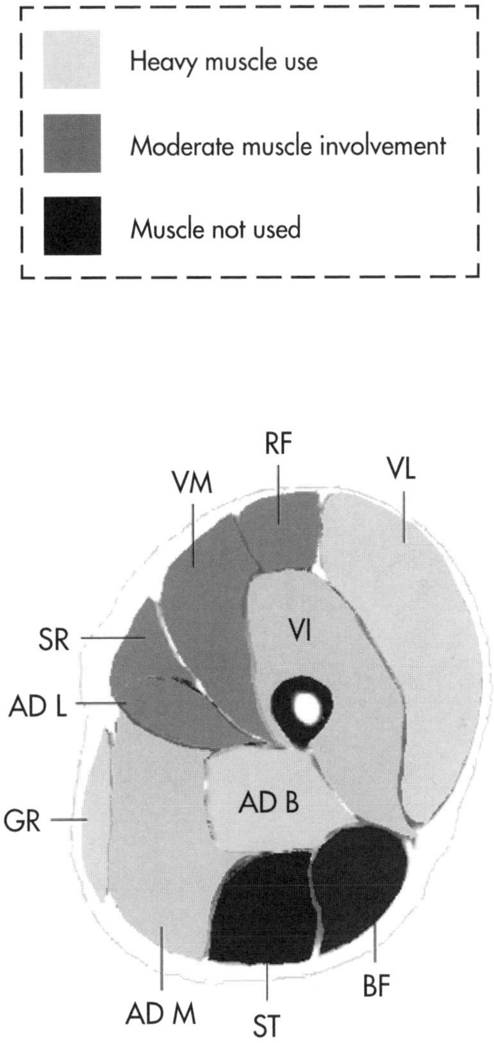

To understand the orientation of the MRI, stand and look down at your right leg and imagine looking into a cross-sectional slice of your right thigh. The cross-section of the MRI is indicated by the bar in the photo.

AD B	=	Adductor brevis
AD L	=	Adductor longus
AD M	=	Adductor magnus
BF	=	Biceps femoris
GR	=	Gracilis
RF	=	Rectus femoris
SR	=	Sartorius
ST	=	Semitendinosus
VM	=	Vastus medialis
VL	=	Vastus lateralis
VI	=	Vastus intermedius

11

OLD-STYLE HACK SQUAT

THIGH

A

TECHNIQUE

Before the hack squat machine came around, bodybuilders used to perform this exercise with a barbell. Sometimes it is incorrectly referred to as a sissy squat. A bar is held behind the body to add extra resistance. Stand in front of an Olympic bar, bend down, reach back, and grasp it with both hands (reverse grip with one or both hands). While keeping the back straight and extended as far as possible, do a partial toe raise so your heels are off the floor. Now, extend at the hip and knee joints to a standing position. Pause after completely extending and then lower the bar to the floor while staying up on your toes with your back upright. Oh, what a burn!

B

OLD-STYLE HACK SQUAT

MUSCLE FUNCTION

Muscle use for this exercise is similar to that for the sissy squat (exercise 12). The entire quadriceps femoris (VL, VM, VI, and RF) is "lit up." The adductor magnus (AD M) is used moderately. Although it takes a few sessions to learn how to do this exercise, it is rewarding because of its great effect on the quad.

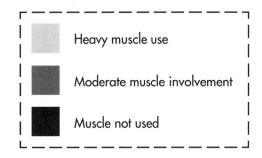

- Heavy muscle use
- Moderate muscle involvement
- Muscle not used

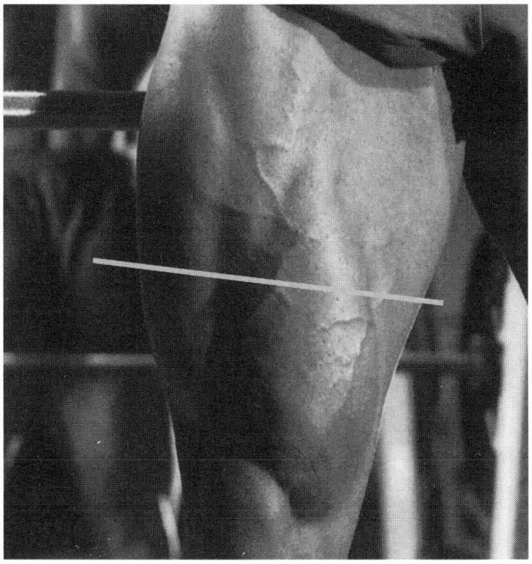

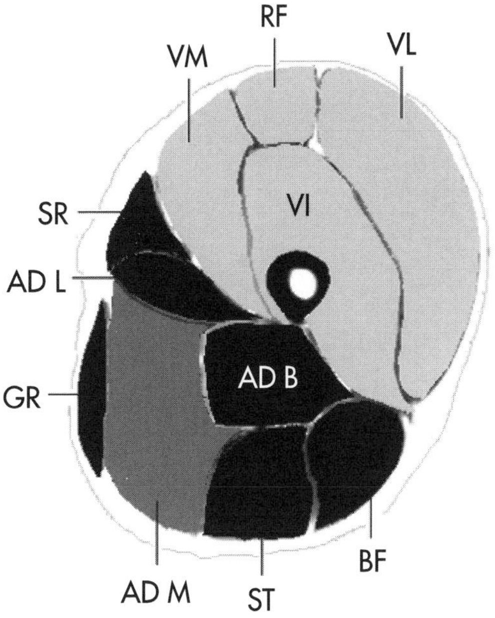

To understand the orientation of the MRI, stand and look down at your right leg and imagine looking into a cross-sectional slice of your right thigh. The cross-section of the MRI is indicated by the bar in the photo.

AD B = Adductor brevis
AD L = Adductor longus
AD M = Adductor magnus
BF = Biceps femoris
GR = Gracilis
RF = Rectus femoris
SR = Sartorius
ST = Semitendinosus
VM = Vastus medialis
VL = Vastus lateralis
VI = Vastus intermedius

12

THIGH

SISSY SQUAT

A

TECHNIQUE

The name belies the difficulty of this exercise. Stand beside a solid support and grasp it with one hand. Now, execute a toe raise, get those heels up off the floor. OK, you are ready to get serious. Descend by forcing the knees way out over the toes and leaning slightly back. Descend as far as possible, maybe until the thighs rest on the calves. After a short pause, get those quads going and return to the starting position. During ascent, remain up on the toes, and keep the torso leaning slightly back. Once you get this down, you can add resistance by holding a plate across the chest/ abdomen with the opposite arm. Do not use the supporting arm, which is for balance, to help in pulling you up.

B

SISSY SQUAT

MUSCLE FUNCTION

All four muscles (VL, VM, VI, and RF) of the quadriceps femoris show full involvement. The three vasti muscles are very active in all kinds of squats. The rectus femoris is not. In contrast to the vasti muscles, it crosses two joints and is sometimes used to perform flexion at the hip. To bring it into action you must pick exercises where the hip is rather fixed—like this one!

- Heavy muscle use
- Moderate muscle involvement
- Muscle not used

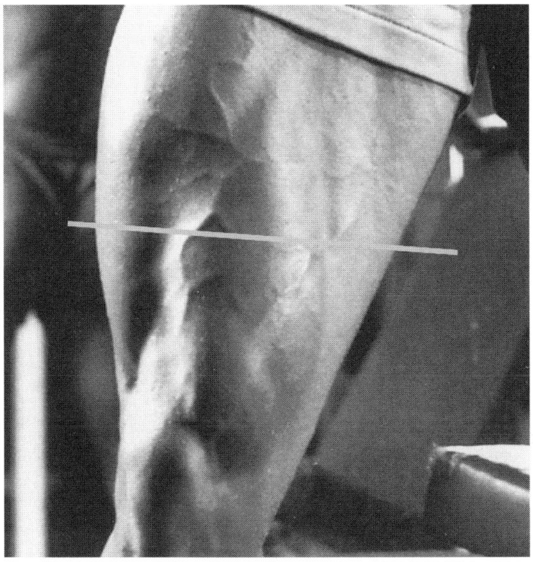

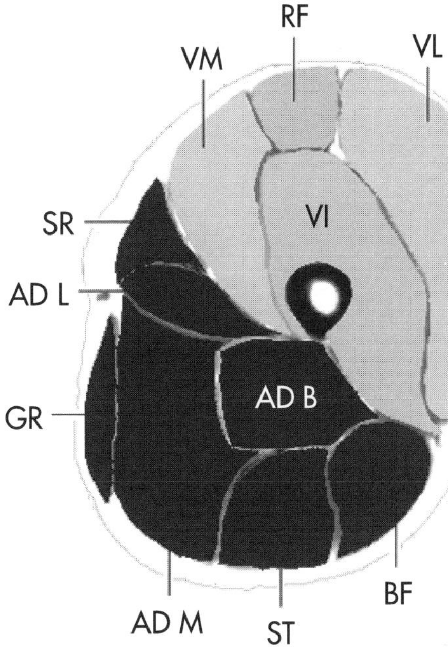

To understand the orientation of the MRI, stand and look down at your right leg and imagine looking into a cross-sectional slice of your right thigh. The cross-section of the MRI is indicated by the bar in the photo.

AD B = Adductor brevis
AD L = Adductor longus
AD M = Adductor magnus
BF = Biceps femoris
GR = Gracilis
RF = Rectus femoris
SR = Sartorius
ST = Semitendinosus
VM = Vastus medialis
VL = Vastus lateralis
VI = Vastus intermedius

LEG PRESS
With Feet High

A

TECHNIQUE

In this version of the leg press, the feet are placed high on the platform, about shoulder width apart. As with the hack squat, you have to slightly extend at the hip and knee joints and move the mechanical stops with your hands so you can lower the weight. Let the load descend until your knees are bent to at least 90 degrees, and after a short pause, use those tree stumps to push the sledge to the starting position.

B

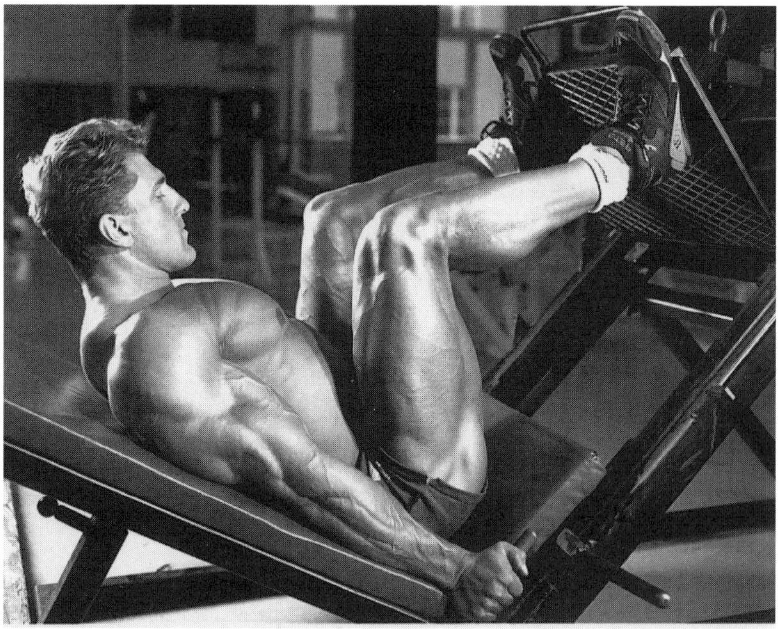

LEG PRESS

With Feet High

MUSCLE FUNCTION

As you'd expect, this is a great exercise for thigh development. It really hits the three vasti muscles (VL, VI, and VM) and the adductor magnus (AD M) and brevis (AD B). There is moderate use of the adductor longus (AD L). It leaves the rectus femoris (RF) unused, probably because of the large hip flexion.

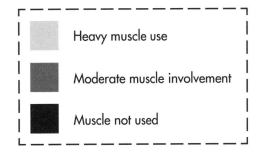

Heavy muscle use

Moderate muscle involvement

Muscle not used

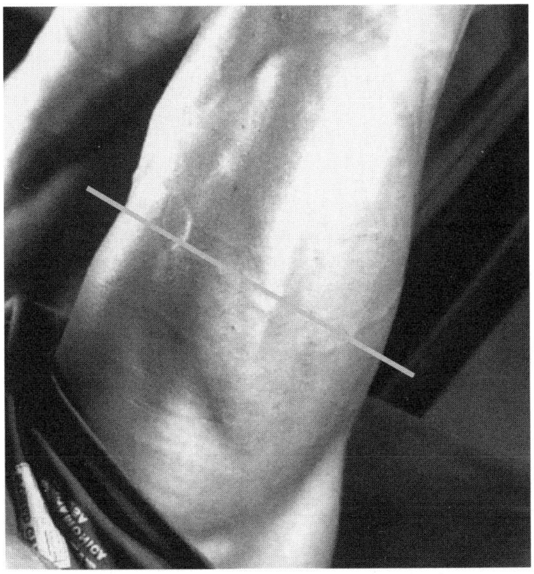

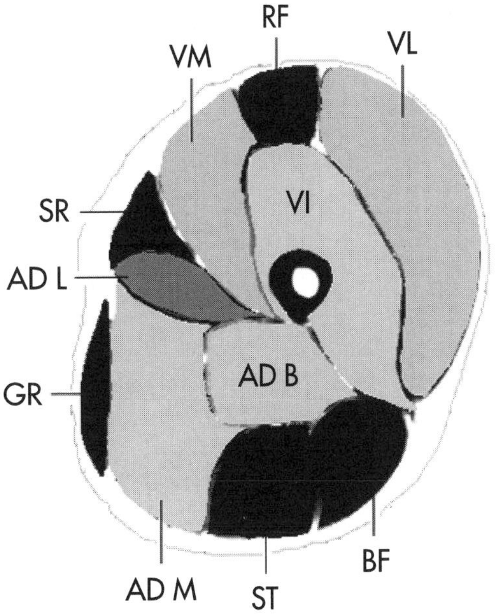

To understand the orientation of the MRI, stand and look down at your right leg and imagine looking into a cross-sectional slice of your right thigh. The cross-section of the MRI is indicated by the bar in the photo.

AD B	=	Adductor brevis
AD L	=	Adductor longus
AD M	=	Adductor magnus
BF	=	Biceps femoris
GR	=	Gracilis
RF	=	Rectus femoris
SR	=	Sartorius
ST	=	Semitendinosus
VM	=	Vastus medialis
VL	=	Vastus lateralis
VI	=	Vastus intermedius

14

LEG PRESS
With Feet Low

T
H
I
G
H

A

TECHNIQUE

This is just like exercise13, except that the feet are placed low on the platform, as far as possible under the hips.

B

LEG PRESS

With Feet Low

MUSCLE FUNCTION

Moving the feet down on the platform when you do the leg press brings about greater knee joint flexion. Again, the three vasti muscles (VL, VI, and VM) and the adductor magnus (AD M) and brevis (AD B) show marked use. The differences are that the adductor longus (AD L) is not used and the biceps femoris (BF) is somewhat brought into play.

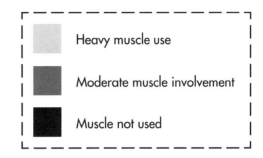

Heavy muscle use

Moderate muscle involvement

Muscle not used

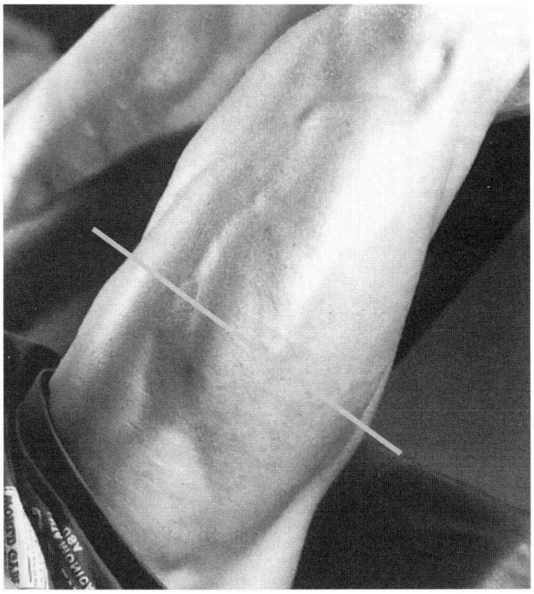

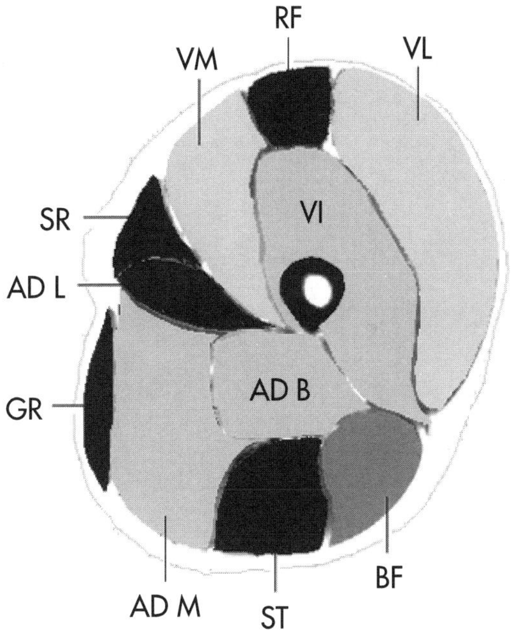

To understand the orientation of the MRI, stand and look down at your right leg and imagine looking into a cross-sectional slice of your right thigh. The cross-section of the MRI is indicated by the bar in the photo.

AD B = Adductor brevis
AD L = Adductor longus
AD M = Adductor magnus
BF = Biceps femoris
GR = Gracilis
RF = Rectus femoris
SR = Sartorius
ST = Semitendinosus
VM = Vastus medialis
VL = Vastus lateralis
VI = Vastus intermedius

15

STIFF-LEGGED DEADLIFT

A

TECHNIQUE

This is like the classic deadlift almost everyone can envision—with some major exceptions. Stand on a box or the end of a stable bench directly behind the bar with the feet somewhat less than shoulder width apart. Bend over at the waist, keep those knees straight, and grasp the bar with one or both hands reversed. The bar is raised in a smooth fashion using the hip and back extensors until the torso is erect. After a slight pause, lower the bar toward the feet, really emphasizing a large range of motion and getting a good stretch. Again, keep those knees rather straight.

B

STIFF-LEGGED DEADLIFT

MUSCLE FUNCTION

The stiff-legged deadlift uses most of the rear muscles of the thigh. The adductor magnus (AD M) and brevis (AD B), biceps femoris (BF), and semitendinosus (ST) show moderate use.

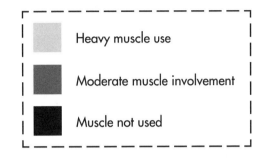

- Heavy muscle use
- Moderate muscle involvement
- Muscle not used

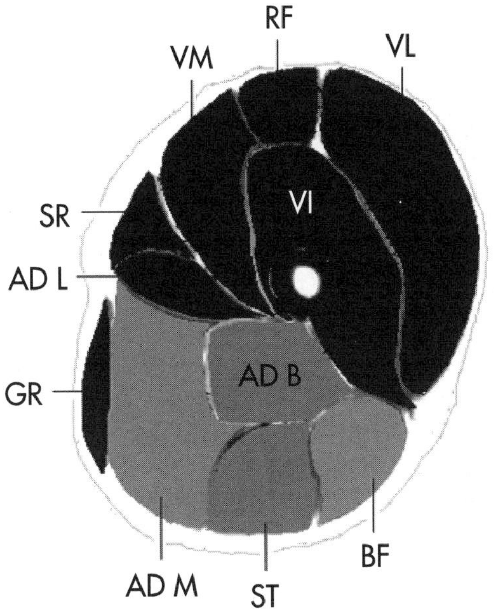

To understand the orientation of the MRI, stand and look down at your right leg and imagine looking into a cross-sectional slice of your right thigh. The cross-section of the MRI is indicated by the bar in the photo.

AD B	=	Adductor brevis
AD L	=	Adductor longus
AD M	=	Adductor magnus
BF	=	Biceps femoris
GR	=	Gracilis
RF	=	Rectus femoris
SR	=	Sartorius
ST	=	Semitendinosus
VM	=	Vastus medialis
VL	=	Vastus lateralis
VI	=	Vastus intermedius

16

STIFF-LEGGED DEADLIFT

With Elevation

THIGH

A

TECHNIQUE

This is just like exercise 15 except that the balls of the feet are elevated one to two inches on a stable object. This adds more stretch to the calves and backs of the thighs.

B

STIFF-LEGGED DEADLIFT

With Elevation

MUSCLE FUNCTION

This exercise moderately works the adductor magnus (AD M) and brevis (AD B) and the biceps femoris (BF). Elevation on the balls of the feet did not increase involvement of the hamstring muscles.

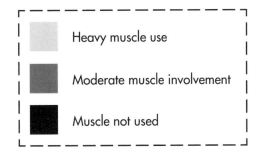

	Heavy muscle use
	Moderate muscle involvement
	Muscle not used

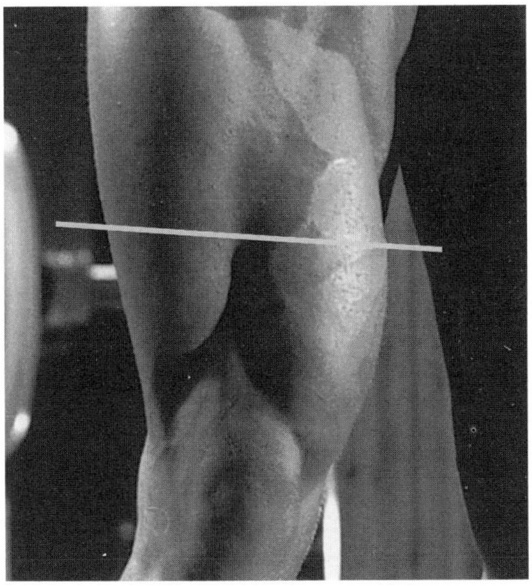

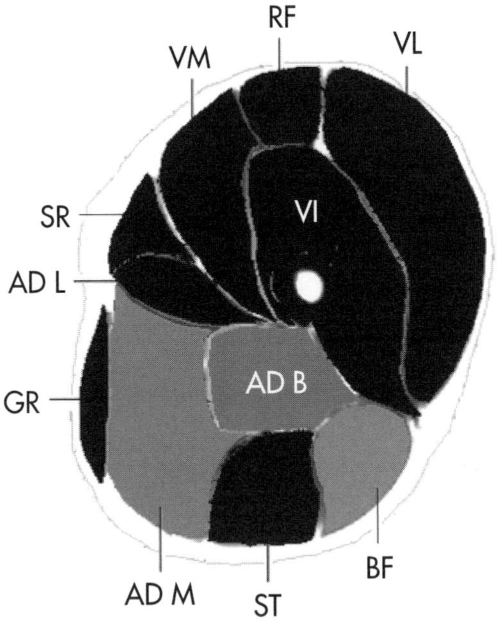

To understand the orientation of the MRI, stand and look down at your right leg and imagine looking into a cross-sectional slice of your right thigh. The cross-section of the MRI is indicated by the bar in the photo.

AD B = Adductor brevis
AD L = Adductor longus
AD M = Adductor magnus
BF = Biceps femoris
GR = Gracilis
RF = Rectus femoris
SR = Sartorius
ST = Semitendinosus
VM = Vastus medialis
VL = Vastus lateralis
VI = Vastus intermedius

THIGH

17

SEATED LEG CURL

A

B

TECHNIQUE

The idea here is to really isolate the back of the thigh. Obviously, this exercise requires a special machine; there are different machines available. The important thing is to keep the thighs from rising when your heels pull down on the bar and raise the weight. So push that padded bumper down on the thighs tight. The exercise is done by pulling the heels toward the rump as far as possible, and after a short pause, smoothly allowing the load to pull the lever arm back to the starting position. Be careful at the top not to hyperextend the knee joint. At the same time, it is important to really stretch the backs of the thighs and enjoy a full range of motion. Also, keep the ankle joint at about 90 degrees throughout the range of motion.

SEATED LEG CURL

MUSCLE FUNCTION

The gracilis (GR), sartorius (SR), and semitendinosus (ST) show marked involvement in this exercise. Surprisingly, the biceps femoris (BF) does not.

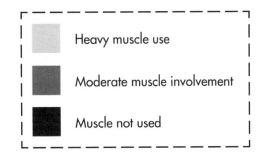

- Heavy muscle use
- Moderate muscle involvement
- Muscle not used

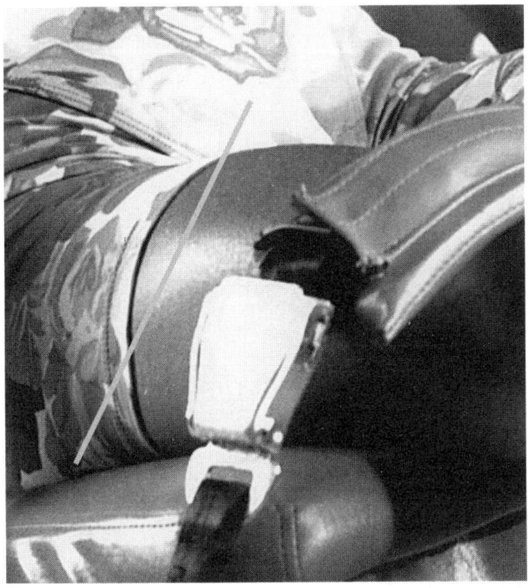

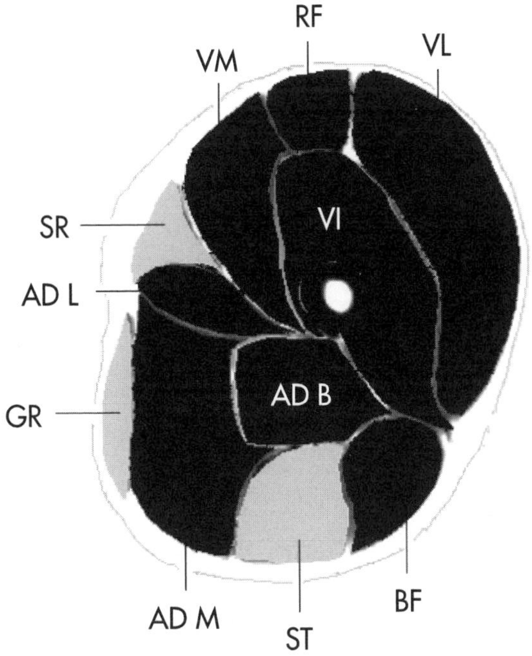

To understand the orientation of the MRI, stand and look down at your right leg and imagine looking into a cross-sectional slice of your right thigh. The cross-section of the MRI is indicated by the bar in the photo.

AD B = Adductor brevis
AD L = Adductor longus
AD M = Adductor magnus
BF = Biceps femoris
GR = Gracilis
RF = Rectus femoris
SR = Sartorius
ST = Semitendinosus
VM = Vastus medialis
VL = Vastus lateralis
VI = Vastus intermedius

THIGH

18

SUPINE LEG CURL

A

B

TECHNIQUE

To do this, pull your heels toward your rump as far as possible without flexing at the hip joint. That is, keep your rump down. Raise the weight as far as possible, pause, and smoothly let the weight pull your legs back down to the starting position. Oh, feel that stretch. Keep the ankle joints neutral or slightly extended during the exercise.

SUPINE LEG CURL

MUSCLE FUNCTION

This is probably the most widely used exercise in the gym for the hamstring muscles. It involves the biceps femoris (BF), semitendinosus (ST), sartorius (SR) and gracilis (GR). They show only moderate use!

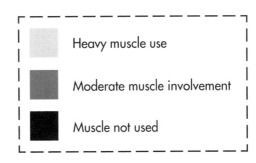

Heavy muscle use

Moderate muscle involvement

Muscle not used

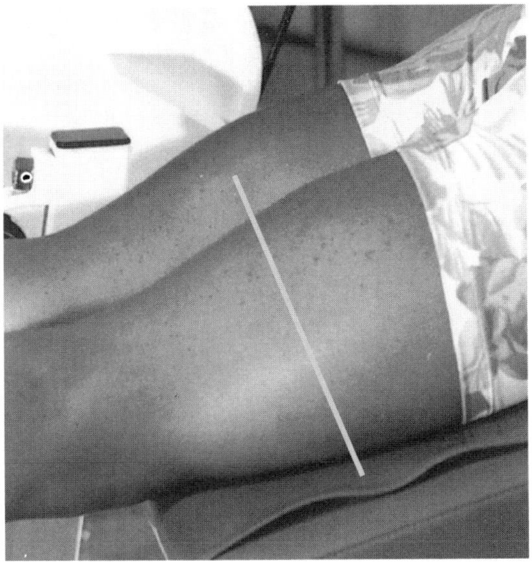

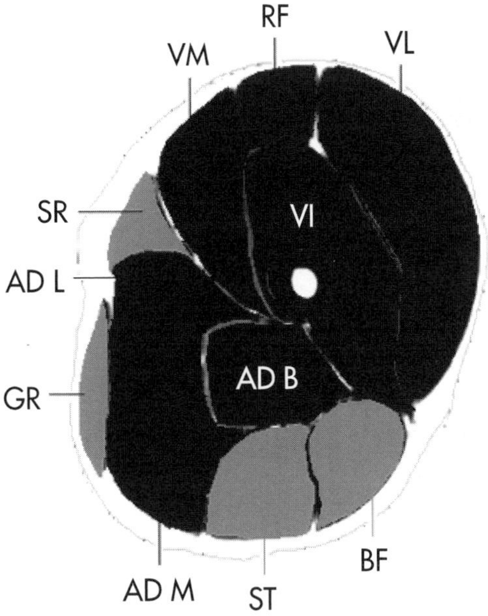

To understand the orientation of the MRI, stand and look down at your right leg and imagine looking into a cross-sectional slice of your right thigh. The cross-section of the MRI is indicated by the bar in the photo.

AD B	=	Adductor brevis
AD L	=	Adductor longus
AD M	=	Adductor magnus
BF	=	Biceps femoris
GR	=	Gracilis
RF	=	Rectus femoris
SR	=	Sartorius
ST	=	Semitendinosus
VM	=	Vastus medialis
VL	=	Vastus lateralis
VI	=	Vastus intermedius

19

ADDUCTION IN MACHINE

A

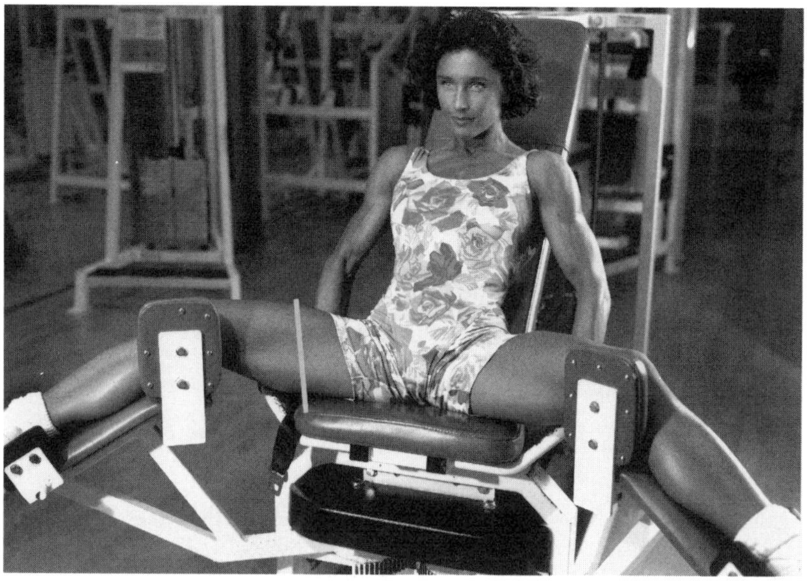

B

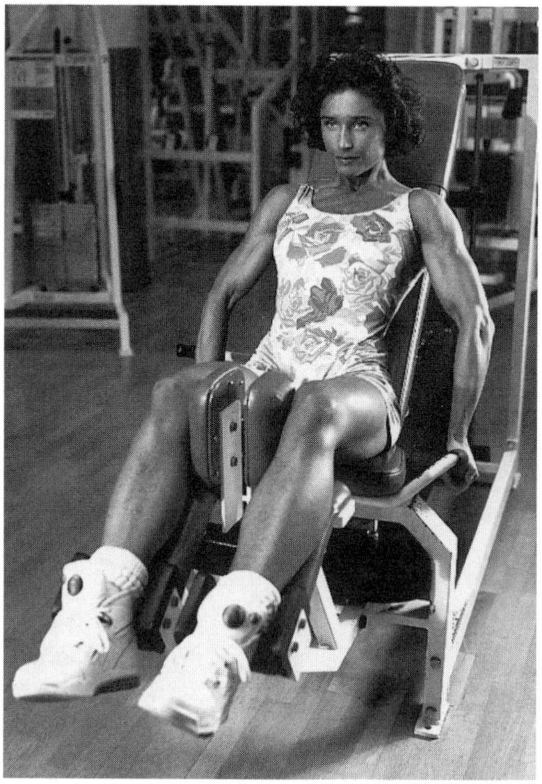

TECHNIQUE

The most difficult part of this exercise may be getting into the machine and then making sure your thighs are not stretched too far apart. Oh, what a feeling. Start the exercise by sitting in the machine, legs apart as far as possible. Now, move the hand lever so the mechanical stop will release the weight stack. Pull your thighs together. Go all the way, then after a slight pause, relax and let the weight stack pull your thighs back apart. Feel that stretch on the inside of those legs; let it go.

ADDUCTION IN MACHINE

MUSCLE FUNCTION

This is an exercise that really isolates one muscle. The adductor magnus (AD M) is heavily involved with some support from the gracilis (GR). Evidently, even big boys should be able to benefit from this exercise by adding bulk to the inside of the rear of the thigh.

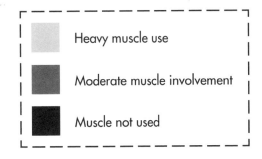

Heavy muscle use

Moderate muscle involvement

Muscle not used

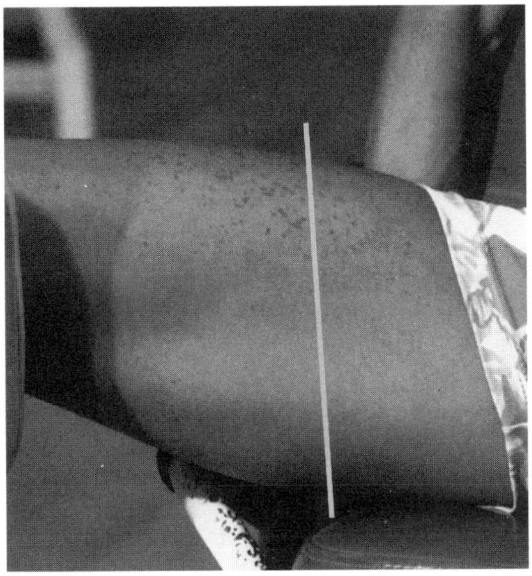

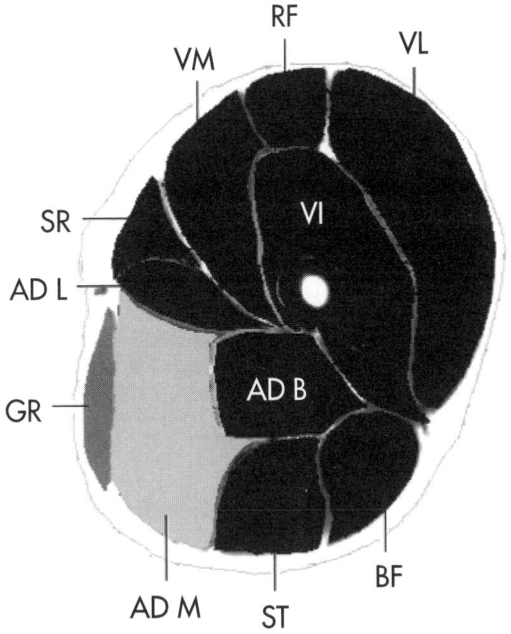

To understand the orientation of the MRI, stand and look down at your right leg and imagine looking into a cross-sectional slice of your right thigh. The cross-section of the MRI is indicated by the bar in the photo.

AD B = Adductor brevis
AD L = Adductor longus
AD M = Adductor magnus
BF = Biceps femoris
GR = Gracilis
RF = Rectus femoris
SR = Sartorius
ST = Semitendinosus
VM = Vastus medialis
VL = Vastus lateralis
VI = Vastus intermedius

THIGH

MUSCLE USE GUIDE

Two Xs denote heavy muscle use; one X denotes moderate muscle involvement. No X is indicated for muscles that show no use during exercise.

		THIGH										
	EXERCISE NAME	ADB	ADL	ADM	BF	GR	RF	SR	ST	VM	VL	VI
#1	**Lunge**	XX		XX						X	X	X
#2	**Seated Knee Ext.**						XX			XX	XX	XX
#3	**Seated Knee Ext.** with toes in						X			X	XX	XX
#4	**Seated Knee Ext.** with toes out						XX			XX	X	XX
#5	**Back Squat** with narrow stance	X	X	X			X			XX	XX	XX
#6	**Classical Back Squat**	X	X	X			X			XX	XX	XX
#7	**Front Squat**	X	X	X			X			XX	XX	XX
#8	**Front Squat** in Smith rack	X			X		X	X	X	XX	XX	XX
#9	**Hack Squat** with feet in front of body	XX		XX		X		X		X	XX	XX
#10	**Hack Squat** with feet under hips	XX	X	XX		XX	X	X		X	XX	XX
#11	**Old-Style Hack Squat**			X			XX			XX	XX	XX
#12	**Sissy Squat**						XX			XX	XX	XX
#13	**Leg Press** with feet high	XX	X	XX						XX	XX	XX
#14	**Leg Press** with feet low	XX		XX	X					XX	XX	XX

	EXERCISE NAME	ADB	ADL	ADM	BF	GR	RF	SR	ST	VM	VL	VI
#15	Stiff-Legged Deadlift	X		X	X				X			
#16	Stiff-Legged Deadlift with elevation	X		X	X							
#17	Seated Leg Curl					XX		XX	XX			
#18	Supine Leg Curl				X	X		X	X			
#19	Adduction in Machine			XX		X						

CHAPTER 5

CALF

THE MRI SCANS SHOW THAT FOOT POSITION INFLUENCES USE OF different muscles in some exercises but not in others. For instance, the standing calf raise targets different muscles depending on foot position, but foot position does not change the muscle action in the seated calf raise. Therefore, if you want to emphasize soleus involvement and limit use of the entire gastrocnemius, you should perform the seated calf raise. Use the scans and the chart at the end of the chapter to target those areas of the calf that need work.

DONKEY CALF RAISE

A

TECHNIQUE

The idea here is to stand with the balls of the feet elevated, so you can really stretch the calves. In this version of the exercise, the toes point straight forward and the feet are about shoulder width apart. Keep your knees relatively straight and your back slightly arched. The exercise is done by pulling with the calves until you are up on your toes. At the top of the ascent, pause, and then slowly lower back down to the starting position. Enjoy a full stretch at the bottom. If you don't have access to a machine like this one, ask your partner to sit on your back, providing extra resistance—as in the original donkeys.

B

DONKEY CALF RAISE

MUSCLE FUNCTION

This calf exercise really taxes the medial gastrocnemius (MG). The soleus (SO) and peroneus longus (PL) are moderately involved. You can use a partner sitting on your back instead of a donkey machine to provide an extra load.

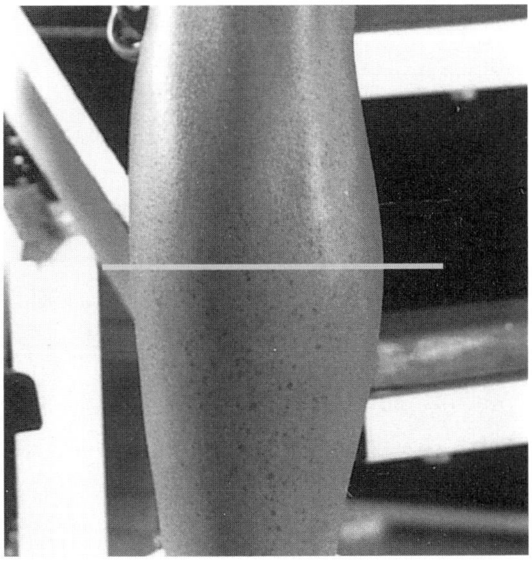

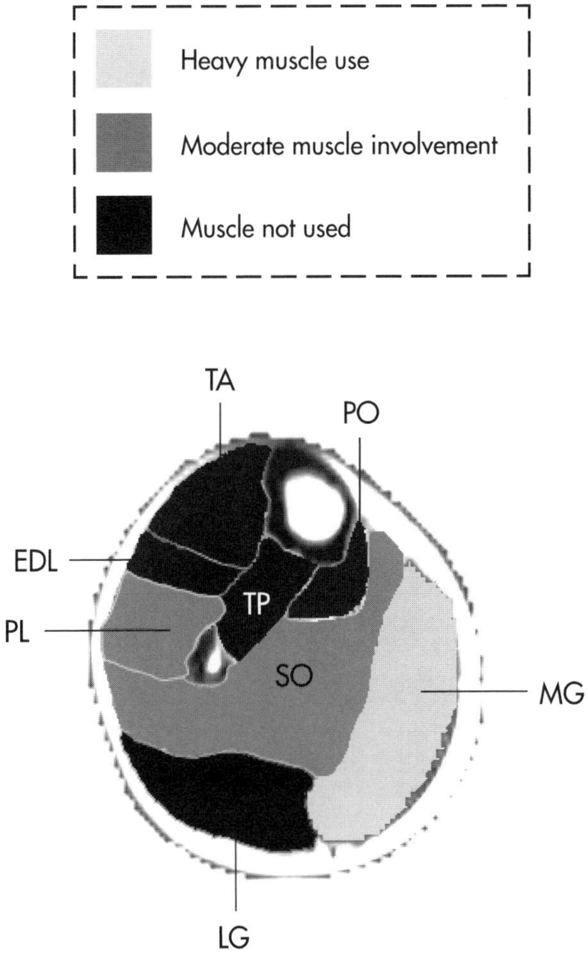

To understand the orientation of the MRI, look down at your left leg and imagine looking into a cross-sectional slice of your left calf. The cross-section of the MRI is indicated by the bar in the photo.

SO = Soleus
MG = Medial gastrocnemius
LG = Lateral gastrocnemius
TA = Tibialis anterior
TP = Tibialis posterior
PO = Popliteus
EDL = Extensor digitorum longus
PL = Peroneus longus

2

DONKEY CALF RAISE

With Toes In

A

TECHNIQUE

This is just like exercise 1 except that the toes are pointed inward as far as possible.

B

DONKEY CALF RAISE

With Toes In

MUSCLE FUNCTION

Performing donkey raises with the toes rotated in involves the same muscles as doing the exercise with the foot held neutral (exercise 1). The medial gastrocnemius (MG) enjoys the most stress, while the soleus (SO) and peroneus longus (PL) show moderate use.

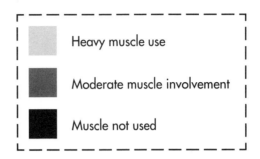

Heavy muscle use

Moderate muscle involvement

Muscle not used

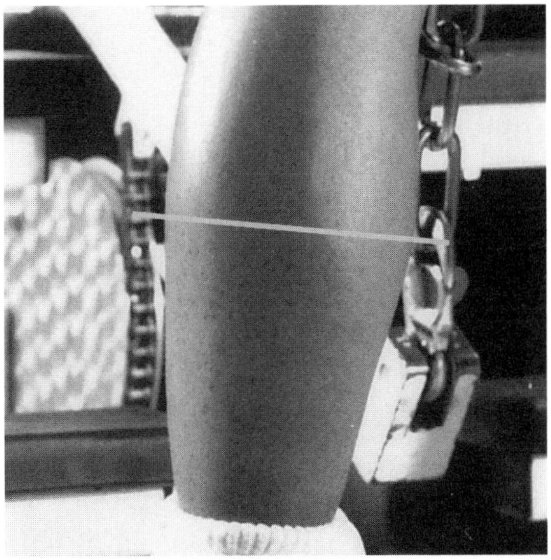

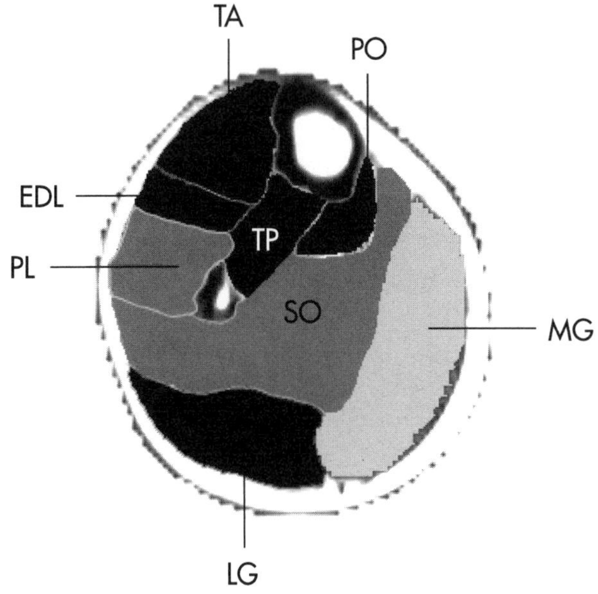

To understand the orientation of the MRI, look down at your left leg and imagine looking into a cross-sectional slice of your left calf. The cross-section of the MRI is indicated by the bar in the photo.

SO = Soleus
MG = Medial gastrocnemius
LG = Lateral gastrocnemius
TA = Tibialis anterior
TP = Tibialis posterior
PO = Popliteus
EDL = Extensor digitorum longus
PL = Peroneus longus

3

DONKEY CALF RAISE

With Toes Out

CALF

A

TECHNIQUE

This is just like exercises 1 and 2, except that the feet are rotated laterally as far as possible, thus the toes point outward.

B

DONKEY CALF RAISE

With Toes Out

MUSCLE FUNCTION

This calf exercise mainly stresses the medial gastrocnemius (MG). The soleus (SO), lateral gastrocnemius (LG) and peroneus longus (PL) are moderately used. Donkey raises, regardless of foot position, always seem to exercise the medial gastrocnemius more than any other muscle.

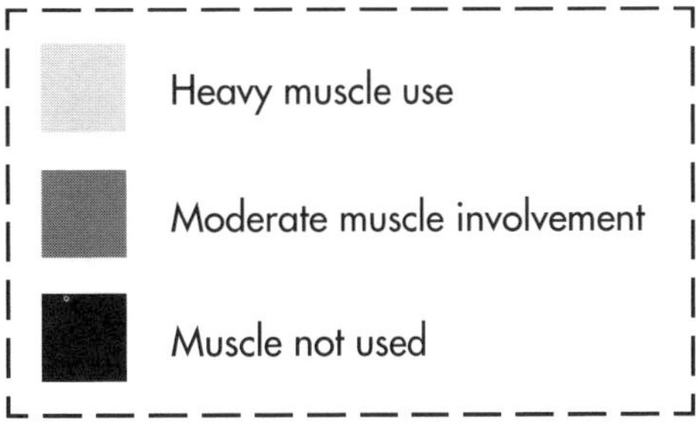

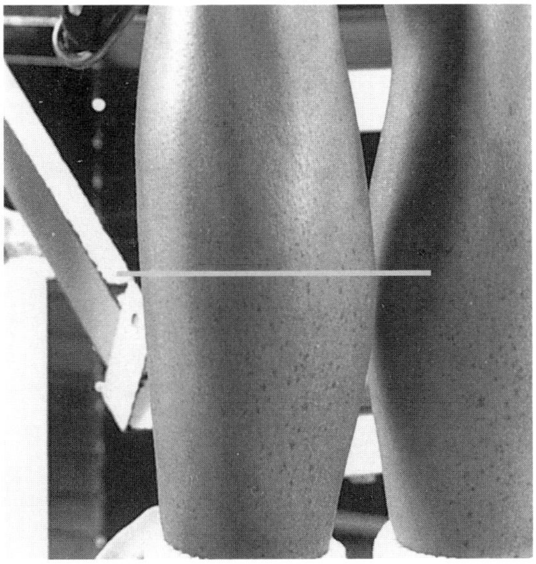

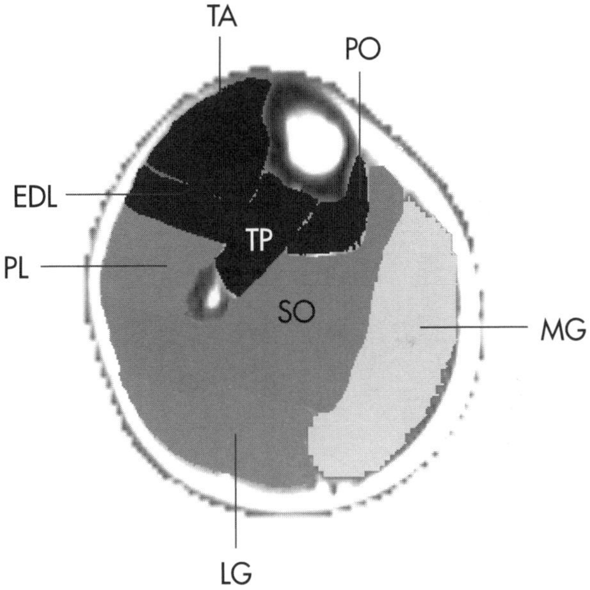

To understand the orientation of the MRI, look down at your left leg and imagine looking into a cross-sectional slice of your left calf. The cross-section of the MRI is indicated by the bar in the photo.

SO = Soleus
MG = Medial gastrocnemius
LG = Lateral gastrocnemius
TA = Tibialis anterior
TP = Tibialis posterior
PO = Popliteus
EDL = Extensor digitorum longus
PL = Peroneus longus

4

STANDING CALF RAISE

A

TECHNIQUE

This exercise is done one leg at a time, to really stress the calf. Emphasize full stretch when you lower the heel, come to a complete stop and then elevate your body as much as possible with no jerk. The only joint that should show much movement is the ankle joint.

B

STANDING CALF RAISE

MUSCLE FUNCTION

If you want to get the calf involved, this is the exercise! The medial and lateral gastrocnemius (MG and LG), soleus (SO) and peroneus longus (PL) show marked involvement. Muscle use should be the same if you do this exercise with both legs. If you tend to favor one leg over the other, however, you should do this exercise one leg at a time.

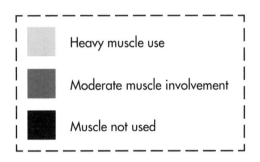

(light)	Heavy muscle use
(medium)	Moderate muscle involvement
(black)	Muscle not used

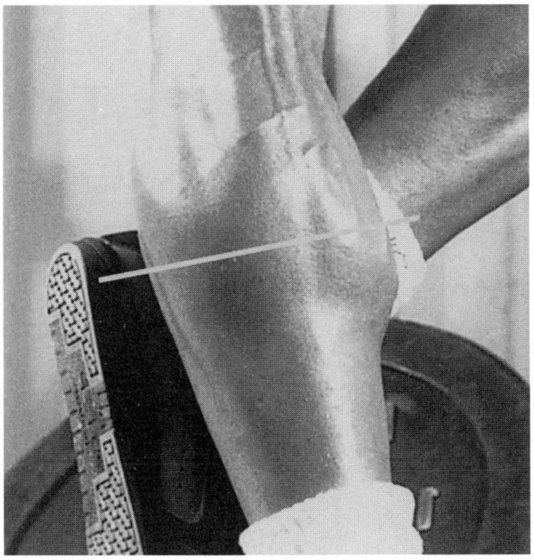

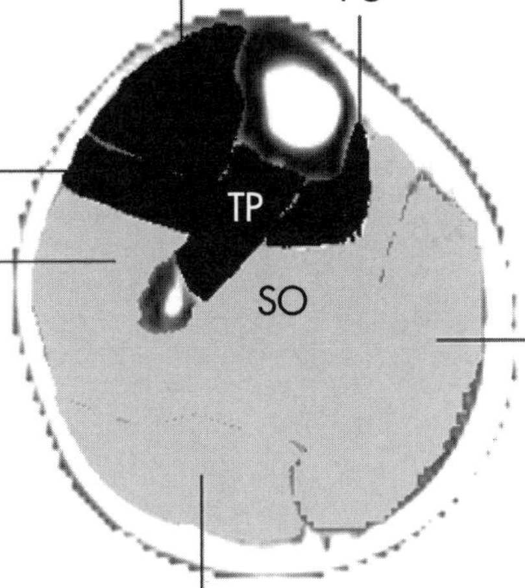

To understand the orientation of the MRI, look down at your left leg and imagine looking into a cross-sectional slice of your left calf. The cross-section of the MRI is indicated by the bar in the photo.

SO = Soleus
MG = Medial gastrocnemius
LG = Lateral gastrocnemius
TA = Tibialis anterior
TP = Tibialis posterior
PO = Popliteus
EDL = Extensor digitorum longus
PL = Peroneus longus

STANDING CALF RAISE

With Toes In

A

TECHNIQUE

This is like exercise 4. Here, however, both legs are used and extra resistance is provided by using a machine. Rotate your feet inward as far as possible. Make sure to adjust the shoulder braces so you can enjoy a great stretch at the bottom of the descent without allowing the weights to come to rest on the stack. Remember, the only joints that move are the ankle joints.

STANDING CALF RAISE

With Toes In

MUSCLE FUNCTION

The entire calf is involved, but muscle use is only moderate.

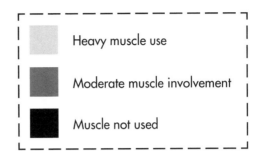

- Heavy muscle use
- Moderate muscle involvement
- Muscle not used

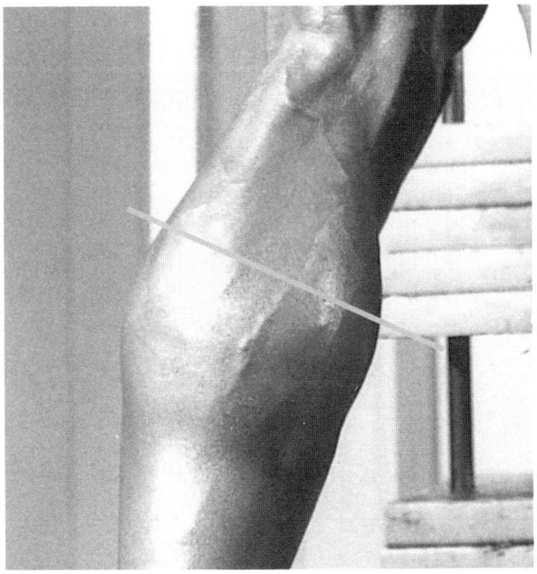

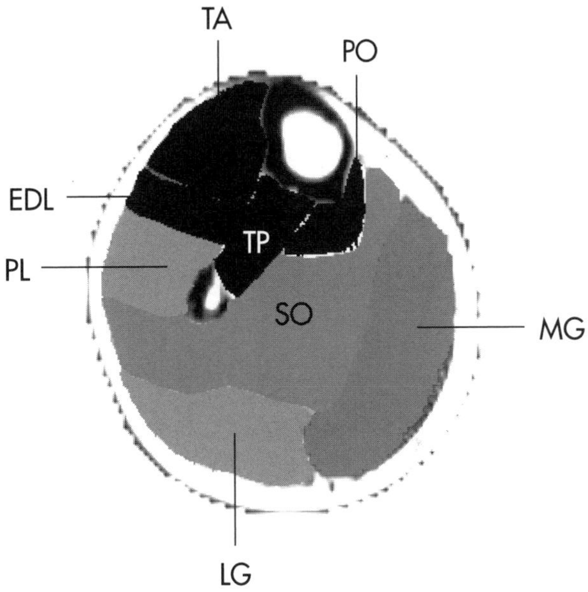

To understand the orientation of the MRI, look down at your left leg and imagine looking into a cross-sectional slice of your left calf. The cross-section of the MRI is indicated by the bar in the photo.

SO = Soleus
MG = Medial gastrocnemius
LG = Lateral gastrocnemius
TA = Tibialis anterior
TP = Tibialis posterior
PO = Popliteus
EDL = Extensor digitorum longus
PL = Peroneus longus

6

STANDING CALF RAISE

With Toes Out

A

TECHNIQUE

This is exactly like exercise 5, except that the feet are rotated laterally as far as possible, so toes point outward. Now, stretch those calves.

B

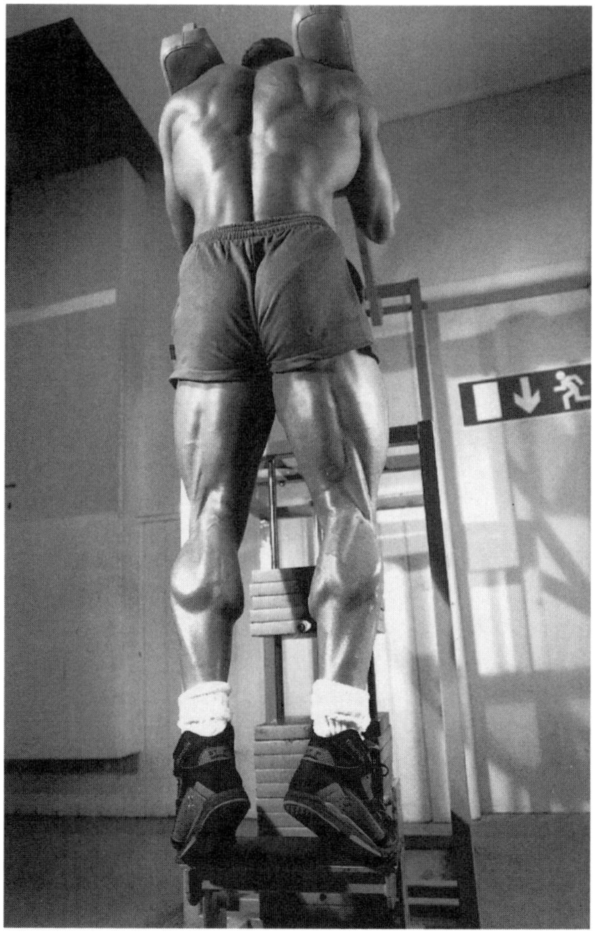

STANDING CALF RAISE

With Toes Out

MUSCLE FUNCTION

This exercise seems to be more effective than the last one, which emphasized toes in. When you rotate your feet so that the toes point out, both the soleus (SO) and the medial gastrocnemius (MG) enjoy marked stress. The lateral gastrocnemius (LG) and peroneus longus (PL) muscles show moderate use.

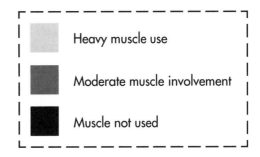

- Heavy muscle use
- Moderate muscle involvement
- Muscle not used

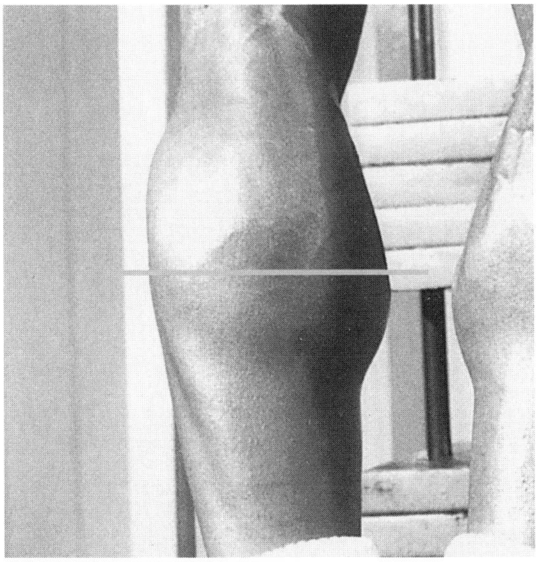

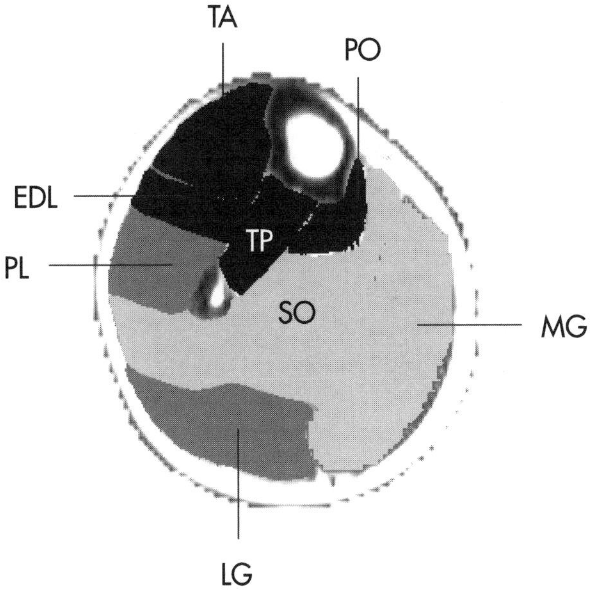

To understand the orientation of the MRI, look down at your left leg and imagine looking into a cross-sectional slice of your left calf. The cross-section of the MRI is indicated by the bar in the photo.

SO = Soleus
MG = Medial gastrocnemius
LG = Lateral gastrocnemius
TA = Tibialis anterior
TP = Tibialis posterior
PO = Popliteus
EDL = Extensor digitorum longus
PL = Peroneus longus

CALF RAISE
in Hack Machine

A

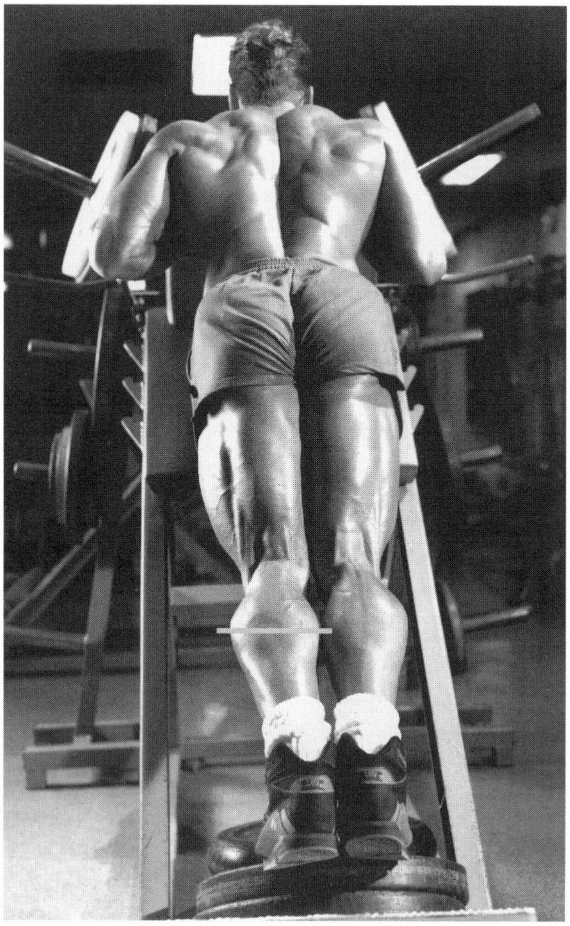

TECHNIQUE

Use a hack squat machine with a block or a few weight plates on the platform, as shown here. Enter the machine backward, so that you face the back support. Place the balls of your feet on the plates, squeeze in under the shoulder pads, and stand erect. Moving only at the ankle joints, raise up on the toes as far as possible, and after a short pause, let the weight push you back down to the starting position.

B

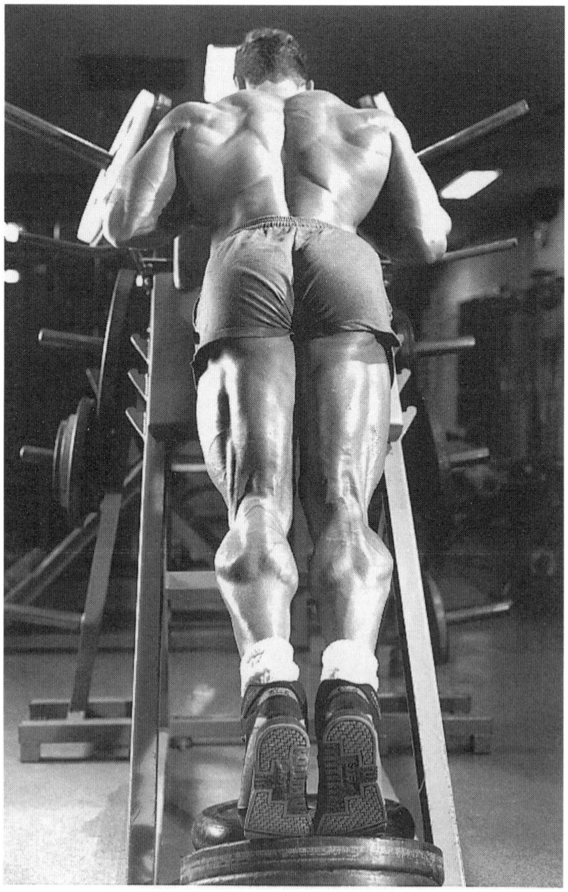

CALF RAISE

in Hack Machine

MUSCLE FUNCTION

This is a great calf exercise. You can hit the medial gastrocnemius (MG) or soleus (SO) really hard. The outside of the calf, the lateral gastrocnemius (LG) and peroneus longus (PL), is used moderately.

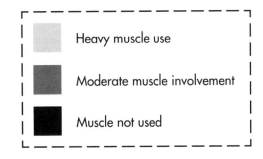

Heavy muscle use

Moderate muscle involvement

Muscle not used

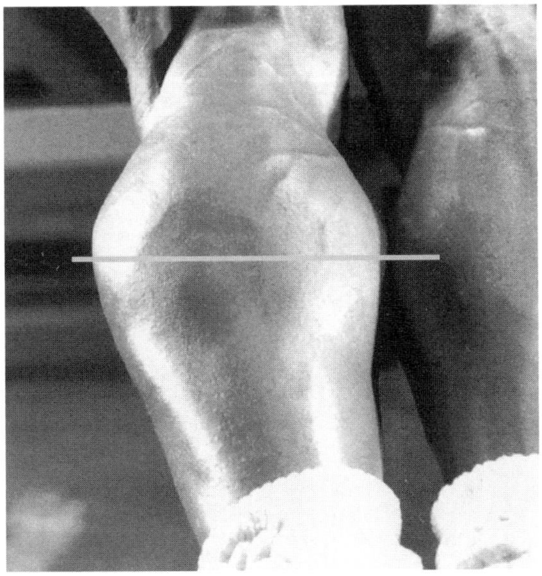

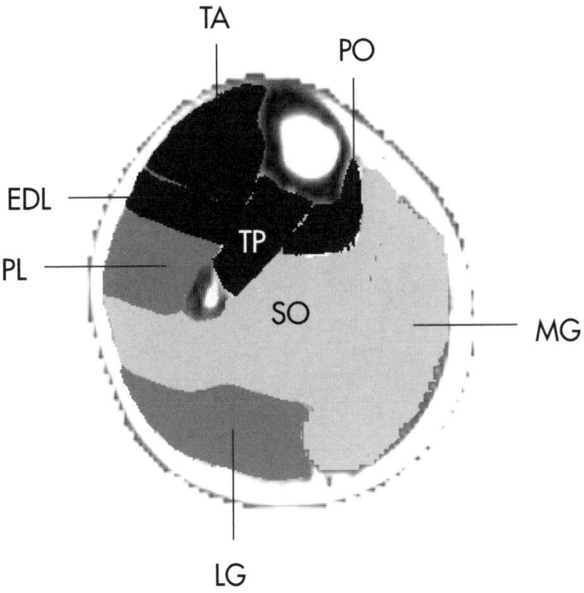

To understand the orientation of the MRI, look down at your left leg and imagine looking into a cross-sectional slice of your left calf. The cross-section of the MRI is indicated by the bar in the photo.

SO = Soleus
MG = Medial gastrocnemius
LG = Lateral gastrocnemius
TA = Tibialis anterior
TP = Tibialis posterior
PO = Popliteus
EDL = Extensor digitorum longus
PL = Peroneus longus

8

SEATED CALF RAISE

A

TECHNIQUE

So you think you've done enough for those calves. Well, think again. It's time for some seated work. Here, the knee joint is flexed at about 90 degrees to start the exercise. The limiting factor in how far the load is lowered should be your flexibility, not the mechanical stop of the machine. Relax, let it stretch at the bottom. Now blast those calves and raise the weight as far as possible. In this version of the exercise, the feet are held in the neutral position.

B

SEATED CALF RAISE

MUSCLE FUNCTION

If you want to concentrate on soleus (SO) development—and not on the gastrocnemius (MG and LG)—the seated calf raise is the exercise. The soleus—and somewhat surprisingly, the peroneus longus (PL)—are heavily involved.

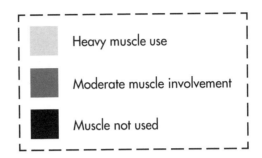

Heavy muscle use

Moderate muscle involvement

Muscle not used

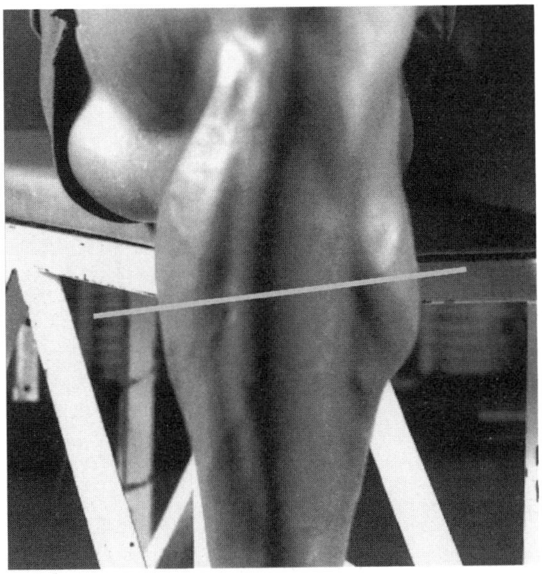

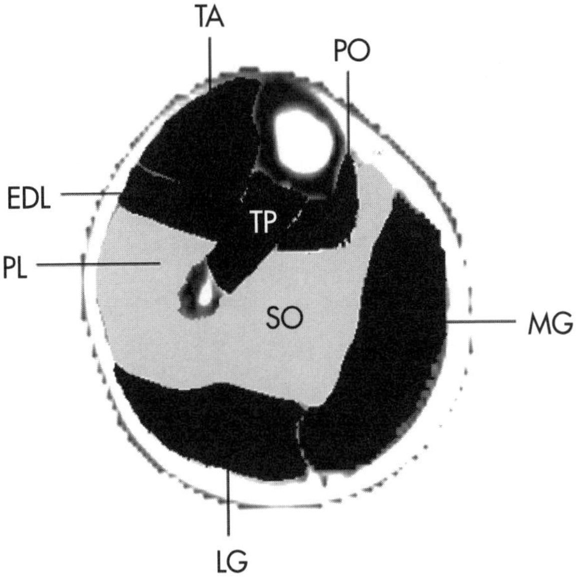

To understand the orientation of the MRI, look down at your left leg and imagine looking into a cross-sectional slice of your left calf. The cross-section of the MRI is indicated by the bar in the photo.

SO = Soleus
MG = Medial gastrocnemius
LG = Lateral gastrocnemius
TA = Tibialis anterior
TP = Tibialis posterior
PO = Popliteus
EDL = Extensor digitorum longus
PL = Peroneus longus

9

SEATED CALF RAISE

With Toes In

A

TECHNIQUE

This is just like exercise 8 except that the feet are rotated inward as far as possible.

B

SEATED CALF RAISE

With Toes In

MUSCLE FUNCTION

This seated calf raise exercise is as effective as the last one, where the feet were in the neutral position. Again, the soleus (SO) and peroneus longus (PL) are heavily involved, while the gastrocnemius muscle (MG and LG) is silent!

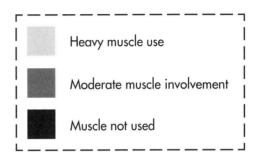

[light]	Heavy muscle use
[medium]	Moderate muscle involvement
[dark]	Muscle not used

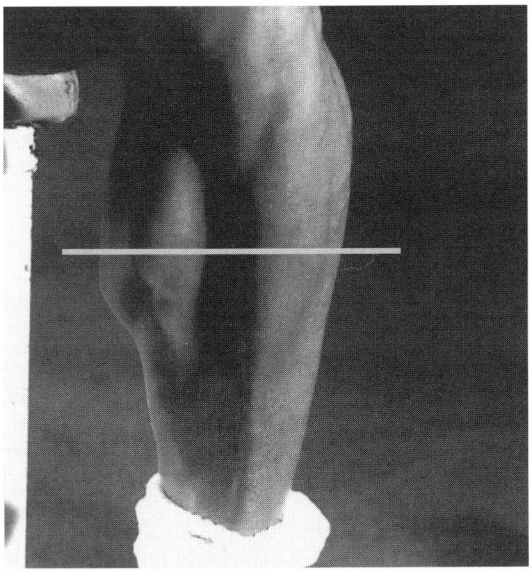

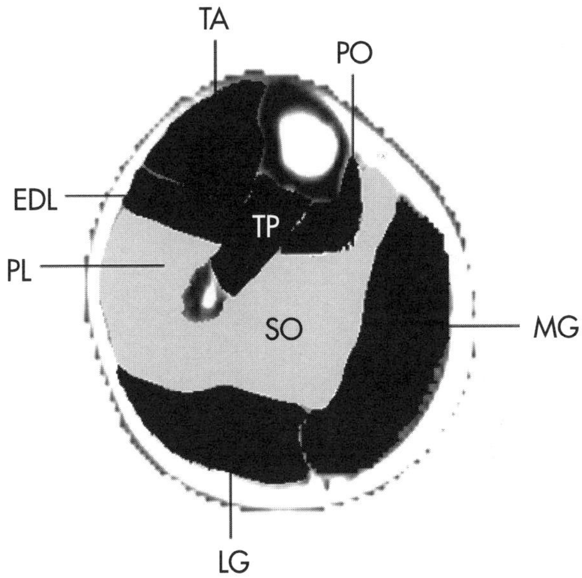

To understand the orientation of the MRI, look down at your left leg and imagine looking into a cross-sectional slice of your left calf. The cross-section of the MRI is indicated by the bar in the photo.

SO = Soleus
MG = Medial gastrocnemius
LG = Lateral gastrocnemius
TA = Tibialis anterior
TP = Tibialis posterior
PO = Popliteus
EDL = Extensor digitorum longus
PL = Peroneus longus

10

SEATED CALF RAISE

With Toes Out

CALF

A

TECHNIQUE

This is just like exercises 8 and 9 except that the feet are rotated so that toes point outward.

B

SEATED CALF RAISE

With Toes Out

MUSCLE FUNCTION

Like in the other seated calf exercises (8 and 9), the soleus (SO) and peroneus longus (PL) get maximal stress. Muscle use is not influenced by foot position for the seated calf raise. You can do this exercise with the toes pointing in or out or straight ahead—it will pretty much have the same effect.

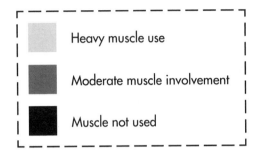

- Heavy muscle use
- Moderate muscle involvement
- Muscle not used

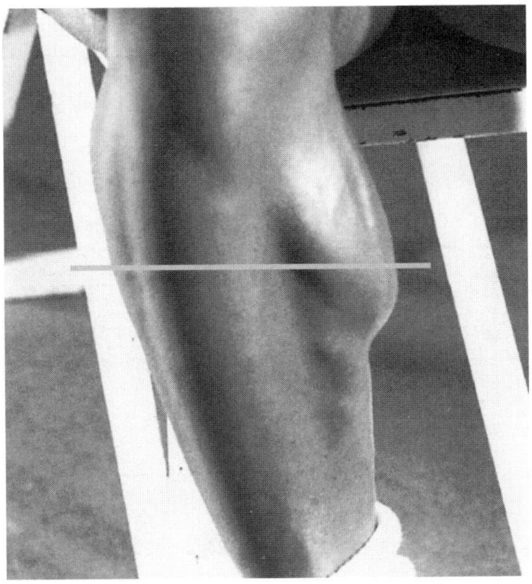

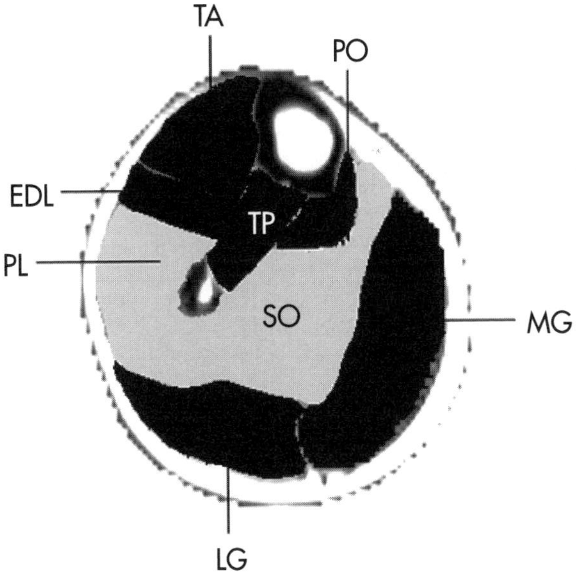

To understand the orientation of the MRI, look down at your left leg and imagine looking into a cross-sectional slice of your left calf. The cross-section of the MRI is indicated by the bar in the photo.

SO = Soleus
MG = Medial gastrocnemius
LG = Lateral gastrocnemius
TA = Tibialis anterior
TP = Tibialis posterior
PO = Popliteus
EDL = Extensor digitorum longus
PL = Peroneus longus

MUSCLE USE GUIDE

Two Xs denote heavy muscle use; one X denotes moderate muscle involvement. No X is indicated for muscles that show no use during exercise.

		CALF			
	EXERCISE NAME	SO	MG	LG	PL
#1	**Donkey Calf Raise**	X	XX		X
#2	**Donkey Calf Raise** with toes in	X	XX		X
#3	**Donkey Calf Raise** with toes out	X	XX	X	X
#4	**Standing Calf Raise**	XX	XX	XX	XX
#5	**Standing Calf Raise** with toes in	X	X	X	X
#6	**Standing Calf Raise** with toes out	XX	XX	X	X
#7	**Calf Raise** in Hack machine	XX	XX	X	X
#8	**Seated Calf Raise**	XX			XX
#9	**Seated Calf Raise** with toes in	XX			XX
#10	**Seated Calf Raise** with toes out	XX			XX

CHAPTER 6

TARGETED BODYBUILDING PROGRAMS AND PRESCRIPTIONS

FOR THE BEGINNER OR BASIC LEVEL TRAINEE WHO PERFORMS NO more than two workouts per week in the gym, exercises chosen should involve entire muscle groups rather than selected individual muscles or muscle heads. Each workout should involve all major muscle groups of the body. Such a standard program is typically made up of a single exercise (three sets of 10-12 reps) for each muscle group. The intermediate level trainee should employ a split routine system (two to four exercises per muscle group; three to four sets of 10-12 reps). Thus, various body parts are trained on alternate days, three to four days per week. This is also true for the advanced lifter adding extra exercises to each muscle group (three to five exercises per muscle group; four to five sets of 10-12 reps), using a five-to-six-days-per-week training regimen. For any category, it is advised to change the order in which the exercises are performed. Although not described in this text, it is understood that programs shall incorporate additional exercises for other important muscle groups, such as the back, chest and shoulders.

BICEPS TRAINING PROGRAM

The standing biceps curl with straight bar and arm blaster (exercise 10) or with narrow grip (exercise 11) uses all three heads heavily. Several standing or seated dumbbell or barbell curls show simultaneous heavy use of the medial and lateral aspects of the biceps brachii with some support from the brachialis (exercises 5, 6, 8, and 9). Performing dumbbell curls with neutral grip will limit involvement of the medial head (exercises 4 and 7). Optimal stress of the medial head, to build "top" of biceps, is achieved by using exercises with grip and/or lateral rotation (e.g., exercises 1-3).

BASIC BICEPS PROGRAM

The basic level trainee should employ a biceps exercise that uses all three heads. Exercises such as the standing biceps curl with barbell (i.e., exercise 10 or 11) are preferred because all three heads show heavy use.

Choose one of the following core exercises

#	Exercise Name	Page	Sets	Reps	Target Area
10	Standing Biceps Curl with straight bar and arm blaster	28	3	10—12	All heads of Biceps
11	Standing Biceps Curl with straight bar and narrow grip	30	3	10—12	All heads of Biceps

INTERMEDIATE BICEPS PROGRAM

Pick two or three exercises for the elbow flexors. Begin with one that uses all three muscles (i.e., exercise 10 or 11). Choose one that emphasizes the medial head (i.e., exercises 1-3). If needed, add the "hammer curl" (exercise 7), which uses m. brachialis and the lateral head.

Choose one the following core exercises

#	Exercise Name	Page	Sets	Reps	Target Area
10	Standing Biceps Curl with straight bar and arm blaster	28	3—4	10—12	All heads of Biceps
11	Standing Biceps Curl with straight bar and narrow grip	30	3—4	10—12	All heads of Biceps

then add one exercise that targets the medial head

#	Exercise Name	Page	Sets	Reps	Target Area
1	Standing Biceps Curl with straight bar and wide grip	10	3—4	10—12	medial head/Biceps
2	Standing Biceps Curl with EZ bar and wide grip	12	3—4	10—12	medial head/Biceps
3	Standing Dumbbell Curl with palm up	14	3—4	10—12	medial head/Biceps

ADVANCED BICEPS PROGRAM

Select one exercise that uses all heads of the biceps (i.e., exercise 10 or 11). Then emphasize the medial head by choosing exercise 1, 2, or 3. Add an exercise that also brings in the lateral aspect along with use of the medial head (e.g., exercises 5, 6, 8, or 9). Finish up with the "hammer curl" (exercise 7) to stress m. brachialis.

Choose one the following core exercises

#	Exercise Name	Page	Sets	Reps	Target Area
10	Standing Biceps Curl with straight bar and arm blaster	28	4—5	10—12	All heads of Biceps
11	Standing Biceps Curl with straight bar and narrow grip	30	4—5	10—12	All heads of Biceps

then add one exercise that targets the medial head

#	Exercise Name	Page	Sets	Reps	Target Area
1	Standing Biceps Curl with straight bar and wide grip	10	4—5	10—12	medial head/Biceps
2	Standing Biceps Curl with EZ bar and wide grip	12	4—5	10—12	medial head/Biceps
3	Standing Dumbbell Curl with palm up	14	4—5	10—12	medial head/Biceps

then add one exercise that targets the lateral head with the medial head

#	Exercise Name	Page	Sets	Reps	Target Area
5	Standing Dumbbell Curl with lateral rotation	18	4—5	10—12	lateral and medial heads
6	Incline Seated Dumbbell Curl with lateral rotation	20	4—5	10—12	lateral and medial heads
8	Incline Seated Dumbbell Curl with palm up	24	4—5	10—12	lateral and medial heads
9	Standing Biceps Curl with EZ bar and arm blaster	26	4—5	10—12	lateral and medial heads

then finish by targeting the brachialis

#	Exercise Name	Page	Sets	Reps	Target Area
7	Incline Seated Dumbbell Curl with neutral grip	22	4—5	10—12	brachialis

TRICEPS TRAINING PROGRAM

Several exercises offer heavy use of all three heads of the triceps: French press with EZ bar on a decline bench (exercise 2), overhead triceps extension with dumbbell and neutral grip (exercise 4) or rotation (exercise 5), triceps push down with rope (exercise 9) or angled bar (exercise 10), or one-arm triceps push down with reverse grip (exercise 12). Parallel bar dip (exercise 15) and bench dip (exercise 16) are equally effective. The long head shows heavy use, with support by the medial and/or lateral head, in exercises 1, 6, and 17. The lateral head is highly stressed in either exercise 3 or 13. The medial head appears to be hard to activate selectively. Once it is heavily involved, the lateral aspect shows similar use or all three heads are brought into serious action.

BASIC TRICEPS PROGRAM

If a single triceps exercise is to be executed, choose exercise 2, 4, 5, 9, 10, 12, 15, or 16, because these exercises depend on heavy use of all three heads of the triceps brachii.

Choose one of the following core exercises

#	Exercise Name	Page	Sets	Reps	Target Area
2	French Press with EZ bar on decline bench	36	3	10—12	All heads of Triceps
4	Overhead Triceps Extension with dumbbell and neutral grip	40	3	10—12	All heads of Triceps
5	Overhead Triceps Extension with dumbbell and rotation	42	3	10—12	All heads of Triceps
9	Triceps Push Down with rope	50	3	10—12	All heads of Triceps
10	Triceps Push Down with angled bar	52	3	10—12	All heads of Triceps
12	One-Arm Triceps Push Down with reverse grip	56	3	10—12	All heads of Triceps
15	Parallel Bar Dip with neutral grip	62	3	10—12	All heads of Triceps
16	Bench Dip	64	3	10—12	All heads of Triceps

INTERMEDIATE TRICEPS PROGRAM

Pick at least one exercise that shows maximal involvement of all three heads. Then add to your routine one or two exercises emphasizing use of selected heads depending on your goal. For example, exercise 1 will mainly stress the long head, whereas exercise 13 will target the lateral head.

Choose one of the following core exercises

#	Exercise Name	Page	Sets	Reps	Target Area
2	French Press with EZ bar on decline bench	36	3—4	10—12	All heads of Triceps
4	Overhead Triceps Extension with dumbbell and neutral grip	40	3—4	10—12	All heads of Triceps
5	Overhead Triceps Extension with dumbbell and rotation	42	3—4	10—12	All heads of Triceps
9	Triceps Push Down with rope	50	3—4	10—12	All heads of Triceps
10	Triceps Push Down with angled bar	52	3—4	10—12	All heads of Triceps
12	One-Arm Triceps Push Down with reverse grip	56	3—4	10—12	All heads of Triceps
15	Parallel Bar Dip with neutral grip	62	3—4	10—12	All heads of Triceps
16	Bench Dip	64	3—4	10—12	All heads of Triceps

then add one of the following exercises depending on your target area

#	Exercise Name	Page	Sets	Reps	Target Area
1	French Press with EZ bar	34	3—4	10—12	Long head/Triceps
13	Overhead Triceps Extension with rope	58	3—4	10—12	Lateral head/Triceps
14	Bench Press with narrow grip	60	3—4	10—12	Lateral, medial head/Triceps

ADVANCED TRICEPS PROGRAM

If you're a serious trainee choosing four exercises for a triceps workout, pick one that offers heavy use of all three heads; carry on using one that emphasizes the long head (e.g., exercise 1 or 6) followed by an exercise targeting the lateral head (e.g., exercise 3 or 13). Top off with one showing heavy use of the medial head (e.g., exercise 7 or 14).

Choose one of the following core exercises

#	Exercise Name	Page	Sets	Reps	Target Area
2	French Press with EZ bar on decline bench	36	4—5	10—12	All heads of Triceps
4	Overhead Triceps Extension with dumbbell and neutral grip	40	4—5	10—12	All heads of Triceps
5	Overhead Triceps Extension with dumbbell and rotation	42	4—5	10—12	All heads of Triceps
9	Triceps Push Down with rope	50	4—5	10—12	All heads of Triceps
10	Triceps Push Down with angled bar	52	4—5	10—12	All heads of Triceps
12	One-Arm Triceps Push Down with reverse grip	56	4—5	10—12	All heads of Triceps
15	Parallel Bar Dip with neutral grip	62	4—5	10—12	All heads of Triceps
16	Bench Dip	64	4—5	10—12	All heads of Triceps

then choose one exercise that targets the long head of the triceps

#	Exercise Name	Page	Sets	Reps	Target Area
1	French Press with EZ bar	34	4—5	10—12	Long head
6	Overhead Triceps Extension with reverse grip	44	4—5	10—12	Long head

then choose one exercise that targets the lateral head of the triceps

#	Exercise Name	Page	Sets	Reps	Target Area
3	Supine Triceps Extension with dumbbell and neutral grip	38	4—5	10—12	Lateral head
13	Overhead Triceps Extension with rope	58	4—5	10—12	Lateral head

then choose one exercise that targets the medial head of the triceps

#	Exercise Name	Page	Sets	Reps	Target Area
7	Standing French Press with straight bar	46	4—5	10—12	Medial head
14	Bench Press with narrow grip	60	4—5	10—12	Medial head

THIGH TRAINING PROGRAM

The thigh exercises involve three major muscle groups: the knee extensors, the knee flexors, and the adductor muscles. Several exercises show heavy use of the three vasti muscles in both one-joint (i.e., the knee extension, exercise 2) and two-joint exercises (i.e., most squat exercises and the leg press). The rectus femoris appears to show heavy use only in exercises where movement is restricted to the knee joint (e.g., exercises 1, 3 and 12). The adductor brevis and magnus muscles show heavy use in several knee extension exercises, the hack squat, and the leg press, where marked movement about the hip joint also occurs (e.g., exercises 9, 10, 13, and 14). Also, notice the modest use of m. biceps femoris and the hamstring muscles in the stiff-legged deadlift (exercises 15 and 16) and the two leg curl exercises (exercises 17 and 18).

BASIC THIGH PROGRAM

For the basic level program, choose two exercises. One should involve the entire knee extensor muscle group, as does the seated knee extension (exercises 2 and 12). Then select an exercise that also involves the adductor muscles—for example, the leg press (exercise 13 or exercise 14). Either the seated (exercise 17) or the supine (exercise 18) leg curl should be employed to train the hamstring muscle group.

Choose one exercise to work the entire quad

#	Exercise Name	Page	Sets	Reps	Target Area
2	Seated Knee Extension	80	3	10—12	Entire quad
12	Sissy Squat	100	3	10—12	Entire quad

then choose one exercise that involves the adductors

#	Exercise Name	Page	Sets	Reps	Target Area
13	Leg Press with feet high	102	3	10—12	Quad + adductors
14	Leg Press with feet low	104	3	10—12	Quad + adductors

To work the hamstrings, choose one of the following

#	Exercise Name	Page	Sets	Reps	Target Area
17	Seated Leg Curl	110	3	10—12	Hamstrings
18	Supine Leg Curl	112	3	10—12	Hamstrings

INTERMEDIATE THIGH PROGRAM

Choose one exercise that isolates the entire quad (e.g., exercise 2 or exercise 12). Continue with a squat exercise that adds some use of the adductors (e.g., exercises 5 and 7). Then pick a third quad exercise showing heavy use of the adductors (e.g., exercises 9, 10, 13, and 14). The seated leg curl (exercise 17) appears to work better for hamstring training than does the supine curl (exercise 18).

Choose one exercise to work the entire quad

#	Exercise Name	Page	Sets	Reps	Target Area
2	Seated Knee Extension	80	3—4	10—12	Entire quad
12	Sissy Squat	100	3—4	10—12	Entire quad

then choose one of the following exercises

#	Exercise Name	Page	Sets	Reps	Target Area
5	Back Squat with narrow stance	86	3—4	10—12	Quad + adductors
7	Front Squat	90	3—4	10—12	Quad + adductors

then choose an exercise that heavily targets the adductors

#	Exercise Name	Page	Sets	Reps	Target Area
9	Hack Squat with feet in front of body	94	3—4	10—12	Adductors
10	Hack Squat with feet under hips	96	3—4	10—12	Adductors
13	Leg Press with feet high	102	3—4	10—12	Adductors
14	Leg Press with feet low	104	3—4	10—12	Adductors

finish by targeting the hamstrings

#	Exercise Name	Page	Sets	Reps	Target Area
17	Seated Leg Curl	110	3—4	10—12	Hamstrings

ADVANCED THIGH PROGRAM

See "intermediate" and select an additional quad exercise. Choose exercises to emphasize variety, so that assisting muscles such as mm. gracilis, sartorius, or semitendinosus are used as well (e.g., exercises 8, 9, or 10). Apparently it is difficult to induce maximal stress to the entire hamstring muscle group using a single exercise. Add two or three of exercises 15, 17, and 18 to target the hamstring muscle group.

Choose one exercise to work the entire quad

#	Exercise Name	Page	Sets	Reps	Target Area
2	Seated Knee Extension	80	4—5	10—12	Entire quad
12	Sissy Squat	100	4—5	10—12	Entire quad

then choose one of the following exercises

#	Exercise Name	Page	Sets	Reps	Target Area
5	Back Squat with narrow stance	86	4—5	10—12	Quad + adductors
7	Front Squat	90	4—5	10—12	Quad + adductors

then choose an exercise that heavily targets the adductors

#	Exercise Name	Page	Sets	Reps	Target Area
9	Hack Squat with feet in front of body	94	4—5	10—12	Adductors
10	Hack Squat with feet under hips	96	4—5	10—12	Adductors
13	Leg Press with feet high	102	4—5	10—12	Adductors
14	Leg Press with feet low	104	4—5	10—12	Adductors

then choose an exercise that targets the adductors with assisting muscles

#	Exercise Name	Page	Sets	Reps	Target Area
8	Front Squat in Smith rack	92	4—5	10—12	"assisting muscles (mm. sartorius and semitendinosus)"
9	Hack Squat with feet in front of body	94	4—5	10—12	"assisting muscles (mm. gracilis and sartorius)"
10	Hack Squat with feet under hips	96	4—5	10—12	"assisting muscles (mm. gracilis and sartorius)"

CALF TRAINING PROGRAM

Whereas foot position will not influence use of different muscles in the seated calf raise, it does in the standing calf raise. To emphasize soleus involvement and limit use of the entire gastrocnemius, the seated calf raise should be performed. In donkey calf raises (exercises 1-3), the medial aspect of gastrocnemius shows selective and heavy use.

BASIC CALF PROGRAM

Choose the standing calf raise with neutral foot position (exercise 4), which involves all ankle extensors heavily.

#	Exercise Name	Page	Sets	Reps	Target Area
4	Standing Calf Raise	126	3	10—12	Entire calf

INTERMEDIATE CALF PROGRAM

Select two exercises—one that uses the entire calf (e.g., exercise 4, the standing calf raise) and, depending on your goal, one exercise either targeting the soleus (exercise 8 or exercise 9) or the medial gastrocnemius (e.g., exercises 1-3).

#	Exercise Name	Page	Sets	Reps	Target Area
4	Standing Calf Raise	126	3—4	10—12	Entire calf

then choose one of the following depending on your target area

#	Exercise Name	Page	Sets	Reps	Target Area
8	Seated Calf Raise	134	3—4	10—12	Soleus
1	Donkey Calf Raise	120	3—4	10—12	Gastrocnemius

ADVANCED CALF PROGRAM

Choose the standing calf raise (exercise 4) for overall massive involvement. Carry on with the seated calf raise (exercises 8-10) to target the soleus. To emphasize the medial aspect of the gastrocnemius, add the donkey calf raise (exercise 1 or exercise 2).

#	Exercise Name	Page	Sets	Reps	Target Area
4	Standing Calf Raise	126	4—5	10—12	Entire calf

then choose one of the following to target the soleus

#	Exercise Name	Page	Sets	Reps	Target Area
8	Seated Calf Raise	134	4—5	10—12	Soleus
9	Seated Calf Raise with toes in	136	4—5	10—12	Soleus
10	Seated Calf Raise with toes out	138	4—5	10—12	Soleus

then choose one of the following to target the medial aspect of the gastrocnemius

#	Exercise Name	Page	Sets	Reps	Target Area
1	Donkey Calf Raise	120	4—5	10—12	Gastrocnemius
2	Donkey Calf Raise with toes in	122	4—5	10—12	Gastrocnemius

ABOUT THE AUTHOR

Per Tesch is an internationally recognized expert in the field of strength training. He is a professor of physiology at the Karolinska Institute in Stockholm, Sweden, where he has conducted numerous scientific research studies on skeletal muscle adaptations to weightlifting. Dr. Tesch has been awarded research grants from several renowned agencies, including NASA, the Swedish Sports Federation, the Swedish Air Force, and the U.S. Army. A fellow of the American College of Sports Medicine, Tesch has published more than 130 scientific papers. He has also served as a regular contributor to such magazines as *Muscle and Fitness* and *Ironman*.

A flatwater kayaker on the Swedish National Team, Tesch has had a long-time interest in applied exercise physiology. He has served as an exercise physiology consultant to several Olympic teams. He enjoys kayaking, weight training, skiing, skating, and reading. His current residence is in Stockholm, Sweden.

Build Your Body . . .

Takes the latest breakthroughs in training science and applies them to six lifting phases to maximize strength and muscle definition. The father of the principle of periodization, Tudor Bompa, presents the very best schedules of training for developing greater muscle power and mass.

Item PBOM0834 • ISBN 0-88011-834-2
$19.95 ($29.95 Canadian)

Loaded with the technique, training, and competition information bodybuilders crave, along with beginning, intermediate, and advanced programs to satisfy every need. Informs serious fitness enthusiasts about how to enter the sport of bodybuilding and helps veteran bodybuilders make the gains necessary to win in competitions. Read *Built Hard* for rock solid information on how to build a rock solid body.

Item PMAN0696 • ISBN 0-88011-696-X
$19.95 ($29.95 Canadian)

More Muscle is a no-nonsense, beautifully illustrated guide that shows you how to build the body you've always dreamed of. This valuable book contains sample training programs plus 125 photos showing you the correct technique for exercises that work every muscle group.

Item PSPR0899 • ISBN 0-87322-899-5
$17.95 ($25.95 Canadian)

Providing cutting-edge information on nutrition and supplements, *Power Eating* is the single best guide to building muscle, cutting fat, and increasing strength in a safe and healthy way. An essential resource for anyone who wants a leaner, more powerful physique.

Item PKLE0702 • ISBN 0-88011-702-8
$15.95 ($23.95 Canadian)

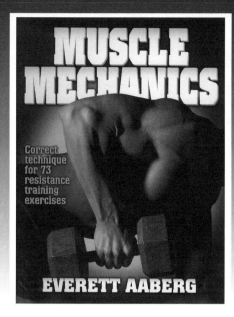

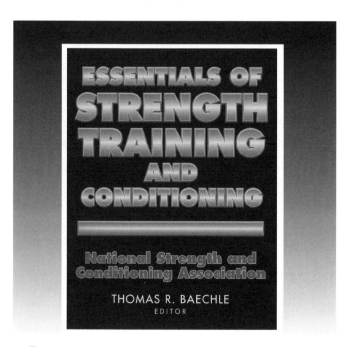